Ralf Kleinermanns

Cubase Vst Macintosh

(:wizoo:)

Imprint

Author:
Ralf Kleinermanns

© Copyright 1998 by WIZOO midi, music & audio technology, Cologne, Germany
Printed in Belgium
ISBN 3-927954-49-7

Translation   Tom Green
Proofreading   Dave Bellingham, Peter Gorges
Layout and typesetting   Uwe Senkler, Hamburg
Cover design   design-box, Ravensburg
Printed by   Continental Printing/EGRA Grafik GmbH

Come On In...

Having spent a number of years testing and working with the finest HD recording systems, I was admittedly skeptical when I held the first VST version in my hands in early '96. However, despite my misgivings, I soon changed my mind about the quality of the software. The attributes that now come to mind are dependability, performance power and versatility.

Don't worry, I'm not going to harp on about how VST on a cheap computer along with a budget-bin audio card is the holy grail of digital audio. This book is not a Steinberg publication, an epic-length endorsement or a glorious testimonial of a true believer. I've simply kept abreast of how VST has developed since the first Macintosh version premiered and had the opportunity to become familiar with the strengths as well as the weaknesses of the software. In this book, you'll find out about both sides of the coin.

The first part of the book is designed primarily to help out those of you who consider yourselves more musicians than computer freaks. What we're concerned with initially is identifying the best gear for your intentions. This section will help you to navigate the treacherous waters of the hardware market and ensure you won't founder when you're configuring the VST computer—in short, it should help protect you from a bad investment.

The second section is concerned exclusively with practical application of the VST mixer. As a VST user you're a studio owner by default, but presumably haven't enjoyed the benefit of in-depth audio engineering training. Based on this premise, the latter part of the book also looks at basic techniques, including how to use EQs, and features some helpful mixdown tips.

Sure, we're dealing with a great deal of technology here, but we'll keep it down to earth and look at all of this virtual equipment as tools—the means to an end rather than the end itself. It's hard to avoid tech-talk in the hardware section, but if it's any consolation, rest assured that the practical section will give you plenty of material on music, sound and creative experimentation. I sincerely hope you'll not only find out about all kinds of nifty new stuff, and also have fun while you're doing so.

Ralf Kleinermanns

Table of Contents

Table of Contents

Table of Contents

A Few Words on the CD Examples and Audio Tracks

On the CD-ROM, you'll find a bunch of audio examples and a folder named Tutorial that contains other Song folders. The following section explains how the files are laid out. If you prefer, you can quickly skim over this section and refer to it later if you have any questions.

Give Me My Examples

You can try out many of the examples described from page 89 onwards via one or even several example songs:

1 If at all possible, copy the complete Tutorial folder to your audio hard disk. Your Macintosh's internal program hard disk will also do in a pinch.

2 Start VST (or the VST Demo software on the CD-ROM) and open the song.

Many of the example songs in VST format were purposely designed to use just a few tracks and effects. Consequently, the majority of Macintoshes will be able to open these directly on the CD-ROM and play them back properly. Nevertheless, you should copy the Song folders to your audio hard disk when you start experimenting with the examples and intend to save the results.

Muted Tracks

Some of these examples feature parallel tracks, a section of which is muted. Don't play back all of the tracks simultaneously unless you enjoy listening to chaos. Spend a minute or two reading the comments on each example to find out what the purpose of the muted section is.

Navigating through Sequences via Markers

For easy access to the sequential blocks of audio, all examples use the brand spanking new VST 4.0 Markers.

◆ If in the upper edge of the Arrange window, several Markers are displayed for an example song, press and hold the 🔄 key to set the Locators and Play cursor as desired. You can also press and hold ⌃ctrl🔄 and click on any position to open the Marker pop-up menu.

▶ To navigate quickly in VST without using Markers, use the numeric key block on your computer keyboard: Keys 1 and 2 to ›jump‹ to the L and R Locator, key 9 jumps to the next Play position. Use keys 3 to 8 to jump to other Locator positions. You can easily define these positions via ⇧ + number key even while you're playing a sequence back.

Loops Make It Easier to Try Stuff Out

If you leave Loop playback mode on and use the Marker function, navigating through these examples is a cinch.

When you're dealing with different isolated sequences, it's a good idea to loop at least one of them. This will give you as much time as you need to experiment without having to constantly rewind a sequence.

Before/After Versions

Two example songs are included for the majority of DIY experiments: The first version gives you the raw material, the second the ›solution‹ or desired end product. The latter lets you compare your results to see if you came up with something similar to the example. In some cases, the solution is also listed in the CD-ROM table of contents on page 169.

Navigating via Window Sets

In the Tutorial folder on the CD-ROM, in addition to the example songs you will also find a folder named Wizoo Window Sets. It features threes preconfigured window sets for the standard monitor sizes:

1 If you haven't installed VST 4.x on your program hard disk, go ahead and install the VST demo from the CD-ROM.

2 Select the suitable file for your monitor size from the Wizoo Window Sets mentioned above and copy it to the folder named Library Files located in the VST program folder.

3   After you start VST, select the file from File ⇨ Open From Library ⇨ WIZOO.

4   Now you have window sets available in VST under Windows ⇨ Window Sets. These let you call up practical preconfigured windows directly.

Use these window sets as a template for your personal window configurations. Add the desired MIDI and Editor windows as you see fit via the appropriate functions.

Once you have edited a window set, make sure that you save the current set under a meaningful name (File ⇨ Save As ⇨ Filetype: Window Sets).

If you want to overwrite an existing window set, simply press and hold the ⌘ key and call up the Original Window-Set.

▶ You can go to Key Commands (Edit ⇨ Preferences) to define any desired key command for each window set. Make a habit of using this option—this is the shortest distance between two points and will let you work much faster, with less effort.

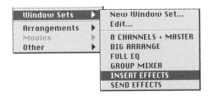

With the hassle-negating predefined window sets, your VST fun factor will increase exponentially.

All Examples Are Included as Audio Tracks

You will also find each example in the form of an audio file on the CD-ROM. You can use the Apple Macintosh CD Audio Utility or any standard CD player to give these examples the once-over. You don't have to fire up your computer when you just want to hear what it is that we're rambling on about.

Finding Examples Quickly via Their Numbers

An example song and the corresponding audio file always feature the same number in the title. These are all referred to in this book via a CD symbol. The numbered examples start with ›02‹ for the simple reason that the first audio track on a Mixed-Mode Cᴅ-Rᴏᴍ is always reserved for data.

▶ All Cᴅ examples that deal with Eǫing were designed for the High-Quality Eǫ. Since this Eǫ is more precise, it is much easier for you to hear the influence of a given sonic manipulation. Go ahead and try out examples with the Low-Quality Eǫ. You'll soon get a feel for which applications the performance optimized Eǫ will do and for which it is less desirable.

1 Programmed for Success

Whether you are an experienced VST user or are just getting your feet wet, you may be interested in finding out a bit of the history of the program. Time for a quick—and I do mean quick—trip down memory lane.

History 101

›Virtual Studio Technology‹—in short VST—is now a core component of the classic sequencer by Steinberg, Cubase. VST debuted in May of 1996 on the Power Macintosh computer platform. In October 1997, the company shipped the first Cubase versions for Windows PCs.

With VST, as a Macintosh user, you're effectively the proud owner of a fully-equipped digital recording studio featuring: multi-track audio recording, an integrated EQ section, effects, automation and digital mixdown gear.

In contrast to other vendors' virtual studio systems, VST was the first program that made a computer studio a feasible proposition for many musicians—one very conspicuous reason being the software's relatively low price tag. The other presumably more significant aspect is that VST lets you work practically and effectively on a standard contemporary mid-class computer without having to invest in exorbitant peripheral hardware.

As far as the latter point goes—accurately termed ›performance‹ by experienced recording hands—the quality of VST is to date, unrivaled. Another advantage of the software includes the realistic user interface, which is a fair approximation of real world recording gear. This factor certainly contributes to the program's easy, intuitive handling. The open concept is also significant as it lets you integrate all kinds of hardware and software upgrades.

In the early versions, users only had a single physical stereo output at their disposal. Coupled with relatively inflexible signal routing options, the shortcomings of the software were fairly apparent, even to the inexperienced user. The ›hard-wired‹ VST mixer was a severe constraint when it came to patching effects in at random locations in the signal chain. The fact that you were unable to route individual tracks to separate outputs put a damper on many a user's enthusiasm.

These restrictions were particularly annoying when you attempted to use the program at a professional level, i. e. in conjunction with a real studio and large hardware mixing console.

Steinberg was well aware of the program's flaws; VST only saw daylight in one release featuring the full version with these unpleasantly conspicuous inadequacies; the company straightened the problems out and shipped an improved version amazingly quickly.

Today VST offers flexible effects routing via send and insert circuits as well as audio routing options that let you separately patch out all essential sub-signals from the VST mixer—provided that you own the requisite hardware.

One of the better things about the program is that it lets you—or more accurately your expectations and wallet—determine at which technical level you want to utilize it. If you have the necessary spare change, you can slap on hardware and software expansions to your heart's content. Virtually anything is possible, from a simple stereo master editor for rehearsal room tape recordings, an 8-track recorder replacement or a center for high-end digital productions featuring 24 bits, 96 kHz and 32 audio channels.

If you're interested, you can check out the development of VST on both Macintosh and PC by consulting the table below. It lists details such as the release dates and special features of all significant VST generations.

Release Data	VST Version	Key New Features
May 1996	VST Macintosh 3.0	◆ First VST version for Macintosh PPC ◆ Multi-track audio recording with routing to stereo master ◆ Audio mixer with automation, EQS, 4 aux paths ◆ Send effects Rack with Choirus, Espacial, Auto Pan and Stereo Echo ◆ Internal Track Bouncing for audio, although with static mixer settings only
December 1996	VST Macintosh 3.02	◆ ASIO driver system for diverse hardware integration ◆ ASIO driver for PPC-AV (Macintosh-internal), Digidesign AudioMedia III and Korg 1212 I/O ◆ Plug-in concept for flexible internal effects expansions ◆ Tun-a integrated as a new send plug-in ◆ Separate effects rack for the stereo master signal, initially with Stereo Wizard only ◆ Track Bouncing now including all effects and automation data ◆ Support of various formats for flexible audio import and export
August 1997	VST Macintosh 3.5	◆ Separate access to all audio inputs and outputs in conjunction with multi-I/O audio-hardware (AM III or 1212 I/O) via a flexible audio routing system ◆ New channel plug-ins: Choirus 2, Electro Fuzz, WunderVerb3 ◆ New master plug-in Scopion ◆ Backup option via DAT stream
October 1997	VST Windows 3.5	◆ First VST version for Windows PC ◆ Features virtually identical to VST Macintosh 3.5 (without DAT stream) ◆ ASIO driver concept with interface to MME-compatible audio hardware and multi-I/O audio routing for audio card with the requisite features ◆ Send and master effects are much like the concept and features of VST 3.5 Macintosh, although this version included a DirectX interface for connecting DirectX-compatible plug-ins
February 1998	VST Windows 3.55	◆ Effects inserts for audio channels, improved interface to DirectX plug-ins ◆ Import of REX files from Steinberg's ReCycle!, flexible audio import ◆ Direct interface to audio cards with DirectSound drivers

March 1998	VST Windows 3.551 (3.55 Revision 1)	• Optimized drivers for enhanced synchronization between MIDI and audio • Most important new feature: internal VST filter with variable High-Quality Mode (Steinberg WaveLab EQ-1 algorithm)
July 1998	VST Macintosh 4.0	›Major‹ update with comprehensive improvements, including: • Increase of the internal resolution from 960 ppq to 15,360 ppq and thus sample-grade precision audio cutting • 8 Send Fx, Fx Inserts of the Pc Version 3.55 • High Quality EQ of the Pc Version 3.551 • Audio Mixer with Subgroups and Fx Inserts (independent of audio hardware) • ReWire function for connecting the VST mixer to the virtual drum machine Propellerheads Rebirth 338 V 2.0: up to 20 audio signals can be routed from ReBirth directly to different VST mixer channels • Marker Track, Folder Tracks • Definable Window sets and key combination • Groove Box (MIDI realtime quantizing with faders) • New MIDI Toolbox • More than 300 new Score features All new stuff in VST Macintosh 4.0 will gradually be integrated in VST Windows versions. However, according to Steinberg, a similar ›major‹ update such as VST 4.0 Macintosh will not be released for Windows Pcs.

▶ For a regularly updated version of this table, check out our Internet Book Support page (the link is listed on page 161).

Which Cubase Version Is Best for You?

When you're contemplating which Cubase version is right for you, be wary of some of the popular misconceptions that have yet to be cleared up. Now that Steinberg has cleaned up it's act and structured the Cubase product range so that mere mortals can understand it, you should find it fairly easy to figure out what you need. Three versions are available for both Macintosh and Pc:

◆ Cubase VST: The basic version, including all MIDI and audio options. If you are planning on using VST in Av mode (see page 59) or with standard audio hardware, don't have an inclination (or audio card) for 24-bit recording and are not in the market for a high-class notation system, by all means feel free to go for this version. It isn't an inferior product and you won't encounter any kind of disadvantages or limitations.

◆ Cubase Score VST: Much like Cubase VST, although in comparison to the rather simple Score Editor of the basic version, Cubase Score features substantially more sophisticated notation options. If you're planning on filling Beethoven's shoes, go for this version; for everyone else who has less demanding notation tasks in mind, stick with Cubase VST.

◆ Cubase VST/24: This is the professional package, the flagship of the line. It is pretty much identical to the ›customary‹ VST Score. Whereas the other VST versions only offer 24-bit quality for exporting audio files, here you can—if you so desire—work in 24-bit quality for recording, importing, editing and exporting. If you happen to own the requisite hardware, this version also supports 96-kHz sampling.

You can also use 24-bit capable audio hardware such as the Yamaha DSP Factory or Lexicon Studio with the other VST versions, but sadly not in 24-bit mode. And there is also the odd specific function for professional audio systems available only in VST/24. As it stands, it looks as if this will hold true for the DSP functions of the Yamaha DSP Factory card as well.

Steinberg ditched ›Cubase Audio XT;‹ it is no longer being developed. If you are in the market for a second-hand Cubase version, keep in mind that this program doesn't have much in common with VST and—in terms of audio—simply can't compete!

▶ Steinberg announced its intention to release a VST/24 update by the end of '98. By then Digidesign's high-end audio hardware ProTools III and ProTools 24 will be integrated in the VST user interface (DAE/TDM support).

Cubase Version	Features	Recommended Retail Price in Germany
Cubase VST	Basic version with all essential MIDI features, simple Score Editor for notation and all VST audio features.	690 DM
Cubase Score VST	Compared with the basic version, substantially enhanced features in the Score Editor, e.g. up to 32 note systems (64 Split) per page, 8-voice polyphony per system. Freely scaleable display and print out, lead sheets, drum notation, guitar tablature and more then 100 graphical symbols.	980 DM
Cubase VST/24	Identical with Cubase Score VST, although with comprehensive support of 24-bit/96-kHz recording, import, editing and export if you own the requisite hardware. Support of specific audio hardware functions, e.g. DSP functions of the Yamaha DSP Factory. (TDM support of Digidesign PT III/24 in the works)	1,490 DM

2 The Right Stuff: Hardware for VST

Particularly for real-time applications such as Vst, it is essential that you select the right hardware and software for your system and configure these components properly. I don't mean to imply that only a high-end Macintosh and the most expensive, sophisticated peripheral hardware will give you satisfactory results with Vst, but you should certainly be aware of where you can cut corners and where you're asking for trouble if you pinch pennies.

Computer Components

As a Macintosh user, you won't encounter the kind of headaches that Windows Pc users have to deal with when selecting the best computer for Vst simply because the Macintosh ships as an all-inclusive package.

Compared with previous versions, Steinberg wisely upped the prerequisites for Cubase Vst 4.0 Macintosh:

♦ Minimum Requirements: ›Apple Macintosh with PowerPc processor 603e and higher, 180 MHz and 32 MB RAM‹

♦ Recommended: ›Apple Macintosh G3 48 MB RAM and higher.‹

Quite a difference, right? What this means in practical terms is that Vst will run Ok on anything but an ancient (relatively speaking, of course) PowerPc model, but it will take a very recent Macintosh model to make the most of the program.

▶ Don't Panic: If your PowerPc features less than 180 MHz clock speed, Vst will still run on it. This said, I still recommend that you consider

In the following section, you'll notice a number of highlighted **key words**. These describe features that come highly recommended for a Vst system. Although you won't find a Macintosh that features all of these, the explanations of these features will help you figure out what you absolutely need for your ambitions and what you can do without investing in an accelerator card or even a newer Macintosh in the long-term.

Processor

The processor, known as a Cpu (Central Processing Unit) in techno-babble, is the ›brain‹ of a computer; much like it's human counterpart, it is primarily responsible for the quality of a system's performance.

The newer the processor type, the higher the computing performance. In terms of Vst performance, this means primarily— more Eqs and effects.

Macintosh computers have, over the years, featured three major processor families. Only two of them are suitable for Vst.

68k Processors

You might be familiar with the family of so-called ›68k‹ processors from way back in the Atari or Amiga days. Although a Macintosh equipped with a 68k processor hasn't been released since 1995, you can still find models such as the Quadra or Lc on the second-hand market.

A word to the wise: Vst will not run on 68k-equipped computers. The cost of upgrading a 68k Macintosh to the level of a PowerPc is unacceptable in price/performance terms. My recommendation on buying a used 68k Macintosh for Vst: Don't!

PPC Processors

The processors of the PowerPc family (›Ppc‹ in short) found in ›Power Macintosh‹ models were the Apple standard from 1995 to 1997. Although, since early 1998, the G3 is the new fair-haired boy of the bunch, its less glamorous Ppc second cousins will continue to dominate the second-hand market for some time.

Just to make things difficult, you should be aware that there are different chip generations within the Ppc family. The early Power Macintosh computers equipped with a Ppc-601 Cpu are too slow for Vst. The lowest performance chip that you can get away with is the PPC-603e processor—the middle generation of the PPC chips.

The PPC-604 and the PPC-604e are the later PPC generations, where the latter is a particularly promising proposition for VST because it excels at floating point calculations, an operation which VST has a special penchant for.

You can expect that the last of the Power Macintosh models equipped with a 604e processor will soon be available at a fair price on the second-hand market. Many users are pining for the newer G3 models, and consider the 604e yesterday's news. But don't be fooled: If you want to get decent bang for your buck and are not into the ›keeping-up-with-Jones's‹ school of technology mongers, definitely go for an inexpensive second-hand Power Macintosh with a **604e processor.**

If you run into third-party processor cards labeled ›604r‹ or ›Mach 5,‹ don't be confused: These are simply slightly improved versions of the 604e.

G3 Processors

From the end of 1997, all new Macintosh models feature the G3 processor. Its formal nomenclature is PPC-750; it is the first chip of the new CPU generation. Although the 750 still carries the PPC prefix, it features a number of technical improvements that provide ample justification for considering it the baby of a new processor generation (see ›Cache‹ on page 26).

The bottom line is that the performance of the G3 processor is better than its PPC predecessors. If you are looking at buying a new box specifically for VST and your budget doesn't force you to settle for a second-hand computer, by all means go for a **PPC 750 processor**-equipped G3 Macintosh—it is a luxury liner among paddle boats.

Clock

Even if you're a computer newbie, you've probably heard that the clock rate is a crucial factor in the performance of a computer. However, you may not be familiar with the fact that there is a difference between CPU and system bus clock:

◆ **Cpu clock:** This is the frequency at which the Cpu can process commands. For Apple computers, this value is indicated after the slash in a model designation, for example Pm 7300/166 indicates a Cpu clock of 166 MHz.

For Vst, your box will need (at least) a Cpu clock rate of 180 MHz. The low man on the G3 computer totem pole currently features 233 MHz, the top dog 300 MHz. Apparently, G3 computers featuring 400 MHz will soon be available.

◆ **System bus clock:** This value indicates how fast the Cpu can exchange data with other components such as the Ram and Level 2 Cache (see page 26) a Ferrari loaded with a Honda Civic transmission, an extremely high Cpu clock won't do much good if the system bus clock is too low—the Cpu has to idle while it waits for the other computer components to respond. The Power Macintosh range features system busses of up to 50 MHz; at 66 MHz, the first G3 system busses are somewhat improved.

Cpu and system bus clock can have almost as much bearing on overall computing performance as the actual type of Cpu you choose. The ramifications for Vst are apparent in the maximum number of Eqs and effects that you can run simultaneously, so...

When you're looking for a Vst computer, you should primarily concern yourself with scoring a box that features a **Cpu clock of at least 180 MHz**—no less. This drastically narrows down your range of second-hand choices. The system bus clock specification comes into play when you're comparing different computer generations (Power Macintosh versus G3) or considering a processor upgrade (see page 48).

▶ Unfortunately, Power Macintoshes with twice the Cpu clock won't necessarily deliver twice the performance. Due to similarly low system bus stats, the boost in performance is often closer to 70%. You should keep this in mind when you're shopping—is the performance that you're actually getting worth what you have to pay for it?

Ram

Ram is the so-called ›volatile‹ memory of the computer. You'll find that you can access data residing in Ram substantially faster than executing read and write operations on the hard

disk. For Vst—in addition to the Ram's standard functions—
Ram is particularly valuable as a fast buffer for data. During
audio playback, data is temporarily ›parked‹ in the Ram to
compensate for data flow fluctuations between the disk and
Cpu.

▶ Here size actually counts. For Vst, the Ram size determines the number of tracks that you can play back simultaneously. If you work with
numerous relatively small ›audio snippets‹—for example, drumloops,
single-bar phrases or effects samples—more Ram is helpful. Vst can
load all of these small audio packets to the Ram and play them back
from there allowing an uninterrupted data stream from the audio
hard disk for other audio tracks.

Steinberg specifies a minimum Ram requirement of 32 Mb
reserved for Cubase in Vst Macintosh operation. To meet this
prerequisite—especially when you consider the ever more
extensive Mac Os versions that you may want to work with in
the future—you shouldn't mess around with anything less
than **64 Mb**.

If you find that, at some point, you want to expand the
Ram, keep in mind that different computer models require
different types of Ram:

♦ The majority of Power Macintosh computers work with
168-pin 5-V Dimms.

When you're buying
a computer, ensure
that not all of the
computer's Ram slots
have small memory
components plugged
into them. With a
couple of free slots,
you'll have plenty of
leeway for subse-
quent expansions and
you won't have to rel-
egate your old chips
to recycling Hell.

DIMM modules can be plugged in individually, but this puts a serious damper on speed. Make sure you buy DIMMs in identical pairs. Plug one component into an A slot and the other into the B slot with an identical number (as labeled on the board). This is the only way you can be sure that the RAM delivers the speed that it is capable of.

◆ The Power Macintosh 4400 requires 3.3-V Eдо Dimms.

◆ The first generation of Power Macintosh models (Pm 6100, 7100 and 8100) work with 72-pin Ps/2 modules.

◆ G3 computers use faster Sdram Dimm modules.

At approximately 60 ns (nanoseconds—the number refers to thousandths of a second), the memory modules in the Power Macintoshes are relatively sluggish. The Sdram in the G3 computers is not much more expensive, but at some 10 ns, substantially faster. Whereas the other memory types can be upgraded to a maximum of 128 or even just a pitiful 64 Mb, G3 Sdram is available as a 256 Mb module, which obviously lets you seriously pile on the memory. The G3 computers are well ahead of the pack in terms of Ram expansion options.

▶ Realtime audio applications such as Vsт have a voracious appetite for ›real‹ Ram. Vsт won't settle for imitations—programs that feed portions of the hard disk to the computer as virtual memory. While we're on the subject, you should make sure that you set the option Virtual Memory in the Macintosh's Memory control panel to Off or bad things will happen. Other Ram manipulations via software (e.g. Connectix ›Ram Doubler‹) are not suitable for Vsт.

Cache

The term ›cache‹ in computer lingo describes a generally small but very fast buffer. The processor loads most commands and data to this buffer and whenever it needs to access these, it can retrieve them much faster than it could from the more slothful Ram.

Vsт transports heaps of sample data during audio recording and playback. This data is routed via the Level 2 Cache, which usually resides on the main board. Generally, there are three options available:

◆ **Modules:** Most Power Macintoshes feature the best solution—slots for the Level-2 Cache. Here you can plug in a suitable memory module; generally these come in 256 kB, 512 kB and 1,024 kB versions. You should be aware that these modules are much faster than normal RAM, which of course translates to a bigger hole in your wallet. VST requires at least a **256 kB Level 2 Cache**; it will do for most applications.

▶ For most Macintoshes, if you're considering upgrading the Level 2 Cache to more than 256 kB, be aware that you'll be wasting your bucks—the only thing the bigger cache will stimulate is the economy. Only in accelerated older models and a few flagship models will the performance be improved a tad.

◆ **Soldered:** In a few Power Macintosh models, the Level 2 Cache is hard-wired to the board. The good news is that VST doesn't mind, the bad news is that if these memory models break down or are too slow for an upgrade (see ›Rejuvenating Old Macintoshes‹ from page 48 onwards), start looking for the proverbial paddle.

◆ **None:** If your computer is equipped with neither a soldered Level 2 Cache nor the requisite slots—which is the case with several Powerbooks—forget about running VST on it.

The latest Macintosh models feature Level 2 Cache innovations that can boost VST performance:

◆ **Inline Cache:** Here the Level 2 cache is packed up and moved from the mainboard on over to the processor card. The processor can thus communicate with its speedy new neighbor at a higher clock rate than via the system bus.

◆ **Backside Cache:** In G3 computers, the inline cache concept is taken a step further. These feature a dedicated bus for data transfer between the processor and the cache (max. 1,024 kB), which also resides on the processor card. The first G3 models used half the CPU clock for this bus. Some G3 upgrade cards available from third-party vendors address the Backside Cache at the full CPU clock rate.

The Power Macintoshes 8600 and 9600 featuring 250 MHz and higher CPU's are equipped with a 1,024 kB inline cache that is accessed at double the system bus clock (100 MHz). These computers are also equipped with the prince of floating point calculation—the PPC 604e processor—so they come highly recommended for VST.

▶ In a conventional Level 2 Cache, an upgrade of the 256 kB minimum requirement won't do much good. If the processor is geared to exploit the substantially more effective Inline or even better Backside Cache concept, you can appreciably increase the performance via a cache upgrade (for example from 512 to 1,024 kB).

Slot Formats

Although the industry cheerfully proclaims Pci is a ›platform-independent standard,‹ the cold hard truth is that software or hardware incompatibilities often cause major headaches when porting Pci card drivers to the exclusive world of the Macintosh. Here's where a basic mistrust of technology, human nature, or both, come in handy. You should never order a new Pci component for the Macintosh on good faith—wait for your local dealer to fit the product in a demo computer and see for yourself if the thing works the way it should.

The majority of Macintosh models seem pretty well-loaded at first glance. But true to our collective restless hunter/gatherer nature, we all find ourselves pining for new and more stuff after a while. For example, another graphics card (see page 46), a faster Scsi controller (see page 38) or a more powerful audio card (see page 64). That's what slots are used for.

There are, or more accurately were, two crucial formats:

◆ **Nubus:** The first Macintosh generations with Ppc processors (PowerMacintosh 6100, 7100, 8100) were based on mainboards with Nubus slots. As a potential Vsт user, avoid these computers like the plague. Why? Because up-to-date Macintosh audio cards—and just about every other expansion—are only available in Pci format.

◆ **Pci:** With the Power Macintosh 9500, Apple introduced the Pci slot format and has since equipped virtually all of the company's computers with this type of slot. Apple's willingness to commit to the format has made the Pci bus *the* standard even in the Windows Pc world. Macintosh users benefit from this development—some Pci cards that were developed for the ›mainstream Pc market‹ are also available at a decent price for Pci Macintoshes.

Slap in an audio card, an additional graphics card and a faster Scsi controller—presto—there go three Pci slots up in smoke. We're not talking decadent luxury here—this is all standard equipment. Macintosh models featuring **three Pci slots** are pretty much the norm in the ›mid-range‹ market and should do the trick for most users. Don't settle for a baby

Macintosh with just one PCI slot; you won't have much fun working with VST.

Peripheral Interfaces

Two near universal standards—E-IDE and SCSI—facilitate data exchange between the CPU and peripheral devices such as hard disks, memory and CD-ROM drives. Different combinations are available depending on the Macintosh model:

◆ **E-IDE:** With the Performa 630, Apple introduced the first E-IDE interface for Macintosh in 1994. Since then, the number of Macintosh models with one or two internal E-IDE busses has been on the rise. When you run across a single E-IDE bus, it is always connected to the internal program hard disk. Often, people talk about ›IDE‹—the E falls by the wayside. In most cases, they are referring to E-IDE, not its antiquated granddad.

If you want to connect two E-IDE disks to a single E-IDE bus (Master/Slave) the same way your Windows PC owning friends do, you'll have to go for the second generation of G3 models.

If a computer features a second internal E-IDE bus, it usually communicates with the internal E-IDE-compatible CD-ROM drive (ATAPI). E-IDE hard disks are generally cheaper than SCSI drives, but unfortunately also slower.

◆ **SCSI:** Once reserved for faithful Apple acolytes, the SCSI bus is now a Windows PC standard. Compared with E-IDE, SCSI lets you connect up to seven or even fourteen devices to a single bus and run these simultaneously (see page 38).

In addition to higher performance, SCSI has other advantages, particularly in studio environments. Many samplers can now swap audio data with computers via SCSI; data transfer between Macintosh and Windows PCs is much easier via SCSI.

Since the Macintosh Plus saw the light of day (1986), every Macintosh has featured an external SCSI interface (with the one exception, the infamous iMac, see page 53). Models that do not have an E-IDE bus on board for the internal hard disk use a second SCSI bus which is substantially faster (see ›More or Less SCSI‹ on page 33).

The internal program hard disk isn't picky, it doesn't care if it has to deal with an E-IDE or a SCSI bus. However, audio hard disks are an entirely different story—to cope with the huge amount of data throughput, you should definitely go for a fast SCSI bus (see ›SCSI Standards‹ on page 33) for the best results.

Mainboard

This is a computer's backbone; all other component cards reside on it. We're not going to bore you and get into what is so great about the ›Tsunami‹ board, what the difference is between the ›Nitro‹ and ›TNT‹ or why you should avoid the ›Tanzania.‹ Besides, it wouldn't do you much good anyway— Apple rarely mentions its mainboard names in their product flyers. Instead, we'll take a quick look at the key questions you should ask about the mainboard when you're buying a computer:

◆ Is the CPU on a plug-in card or is it hard-wired? Only the plug-in version lets you upgrade your box with a better processor card at a later date without a ridiculous amount of hassle.

◆ How many RAM slots are available? Figure out what this translates to in terms of maximum RAM upgrade and ask yourself if this figure will meet future requirements.

◆ Are there enough PCI slots for up-to-date expansion cards on board?

◆ What type of peripheral interfaces (SCSI/E-IDE) are included and how many of these are there?

Be sure to take a long, hard look at these shopping criteria— in contrast to other computer component upgrades, swapping the entire mainboard usually doesn't pay.

Audio Data Disk

I highly recommend that you invest in at least one separate SCSI hard disk for recording and storing audio data. When it comes to the performance and reliability of your VST system, the involved components are decisive factors. Not only are the hard disks important, but also how they communicate with the computer via so-called ›SCSI Controllers‹ (see page 33).

Data Load and Throughput

To understand the technicalities of the components involved in storing and transporting data, you should take a close look at the following two items:

Data Load

When you're working with digital audio data in CD quality (44.1 kHz, 16 bits), you can generally rely on the rule of thumb, ›1 minute of stereo signal = 10 MB of data.‹ For a 1-minute mono track, you need 5 MB worth of hard disk real estate. Check out the table below to find out the amount of memory capacity required for different numbers of tracks and recordings of different lengths.

No. of Tracks	per 1 Minute	per 5 Minutes	per 10 Minutes
1	5 MB	25 MB	50 MB
2	10 MB	50 MB	100 MB
4	20 MB	100 MB	200 MB
8	40 MB	200 MB	400 MB
16	80 MB	400 MB	800 MB
24	120 MB	600 MB	1.2 GB
32	160 MB	800 MB	1.6 GB

Data Throughput

Digital audio data requires more than just hard disk resources, it also has to be transported back and forth between the disk and the computer at an appropriate speed. Here too, it's pretty easy to figure out what the requirements are:

♦ 1 minute = 60 seconds = 5 MB of data

◆ 1 second = 5 Mв of data / 60 seconds = approx. 83.3 KB of data per second

For instance if you want Vsт to play back ten full audio tracks simultaneously, according to this formula, you'll need a data throughput rate of at least 10×83.3 kB = approx. 0.84 Mв/s. As with any best-case scenario, this figure is a tad too optimistic. A few other factors come into play that slow the process down. In practice, the value will be some 20 % higher, i. e. 1.2 to 1.4 Mв/s.

When you're comparing product flyers, ensure you take a close look at the type of specification. You might get the sneaking suspicion that some of this tech-talk is designed to confuse the consumer:

◆ **Burst Speed/Peak:** If you come across these terms or the even more vague description ›Data Throughput, you can safely assume that they're describing the ideal value, the best performance the disk or controller can deliver under climate-controlled, environmentally sterile operating conditions at the Nasa Space Center.

◆ **Sustained Throughput/Low Peak:** These terms describe the lowest guaranteed value, i. e. the performance of the disk or controller under the worst possible conditions such as when you actually expect your system to compute something.

These two values differ dramatically. Don't fall into the trap of comparing apples with oranges: The performance of a system when the stars are in perfect alignment is not what you should be concerned with when you're dealing with an audio application.

The second value—the less thrilling of the two—is decisive. It will tell you how many audio tracks your setup will play back reliably before your system starts hiccuping.

Scsi Standards

Not all flavours of Scsi are created equal. There are several generations and specifications that differ according to the type of interface and maximum possible data throughput.

◆ **Standard:** Also called ›Narrow,‹ it is the granddad among standards; it works with an 8-bit bus width and at a speed of 5 MHz. Its theoretical threshold lies at 5 Mb/s.

◆ **Fast:** Like Standard, just with double the clock frequency—10 MHz. Theoretically, throughput rates of up to 10 Mb/s are possible.

◆ **Ultra** doubles the clock again to 20 MHz and thus has a theoretical limit of 20 Mb/s.

◆ **Wide** is identical to Fast, but with double the bus width (16 Bit). Its throughput is the same as Ultra.

◆ **Ultra Wide** is identical to Ultra but with double the bus width (16 Bit). The throughput limit of this standard is 40 Mb/s.

◆ **Ultra 2:** Same as Ultra Wide with again twice the clock rate (40 MHz), which hikes the limit up to 80 Mb/s.

Scsi specifications can be likened to a modular system: The two bus widths of 8 or 16 bits are combined with clock rates of 5, 10, 20 or 40 MHz, and each ›step up‹ in one of these two specs doubles (theoretically) the maximum throughput. Exponential growth is hip in the Scsi world.

These Scsi specifications always refer to the theoretical or ideal value for data throughput. In practice, these values do not translate to nearly the level of performance that you might be led to believe you should expect.

More or Less Scsi?

You're faced with a seemingly impenetrable maze of bus widths, clock rates and throughput rates. Which Scsi standard serves your purposes best? We'll answer this question in this section. But first we'll look at a more pressing matter: Are you free to choose any standard?

Not really: Depending on personal preference and earnings potential, you are free to choose any audio hard disk at your local computer corner shop, but there is a component that actually narrows your choices down—the ›Scsi Controller‹ or ›Scsi Host Adapter.‹

This computer component controls the data stream to/from the connected Scsi devices. It is either integrated on the mainboard or plugged into the computer in card format. This means that you have to select a computer that is equipped with a high-performance Scsi controller or install an additional controller. The latter option is, of course, only possible if your Macintosh has a free Pci slot.

▶ The Scsi controller should be as least as fast as the connected disks. Otherwise, you'll end up with a ›bottleneck‹ in the data stream and even the latest, most expensive hard disk won't perform any better than an ancient bargain bin leftover.

Some of the Scsi standards that we mentioned didn't gain a foothold in the market, others are, at this point in time, considered relatively exotic. You're left with a couple of hand-picked standards that will get the job done for all audio applications:

◆ **Standard Scsi:** The external Scsi interfaces of all Macintoshes work with this mode—which is a crying shame, because it is obsolete. Experience has shown that the actual throughput is somewhere in the 3.5 Mb/s range. With a bit of luck and a fast disk, this will suffice for approximately twenty audio playback tracks.

◆ **Fast Scsi:** This is a decent Scsi standard and presumably the most common. All Macintosh models with two Scsi busses use the Fast standard for the internal Scsi interface. Generally, you can expect throughput of some 7.5 Mb/s, which will definitely do the trick for 32 audio tracks in 16-bit quality. If you own one of these computers, be sure to work with an internal audio hard disk.

▶ If you own a Macintosh model featuring two internal E-IDE busses and are on a tight budget, you can use an E-IDE disk for audio recording.

At some 6 MB/s, throughput is less than that of a Fast SCSI bus, but still higher than the external Standard SCSI interface. Here too, you should reserve a separate E-IDE disk for audio. As an acceptable trade-off, you could pass on the internal ATAPI CD-ROM drive.

◆ **Ultra (Wide):** If you're one of those forward-thinking folks who has a watchful eye on future developments, want to be prepared for 24-bit/96-kHz recording, and are in the enviable position that money doesn't matter, feel free to drop an Ultra or even Ultra Wide SCSI controller card in your Macintosh. Ultra Wide, in particular, is winning a wide following. You should keep in mind that none of the currently available hard disks can even come close to pushing the limits of these standards.

Even if you have nothing but the best in mind for your treasured VST computer, controllers that are faster than Ultra Wide (Ultra 2 SCSI) are probably a bit over the top. At the current state of technology, these substantially more expensive SCSI controllers are only a sound investment if you work with digital video applications

▶ For high-end audio applications, you should cool your heels until the next generation of technology called ›Firewire‹ (IEEE 1394) is released. This serial protocol delivers substantially higher throughput (approx. 150 MB/s), up to 63 devices per bus, automatic ID configuration, self-termination and the option of connecting devices while the system is up and running. These features should put an end to many of today's SCSI related problems.

Selecting an Audio Hard Disk

Once you know what kind of hard disk controller your Macintosh is equipped with, you'll have to give it a suitable audio hard disk to control. Keep the following in mind when you're writing your shopping list:

Ensure that the disk's specs do not refer to ›thermal calibration.‹ If you run across this term, be prepared to encounter audio glitches. Fortunately, Darwinism reigns with an iron fist in the hardware world and these disks have been relegated to near-oblivion.

Speed

You should take a close look at the minimum data through-put specifications mentioned in the hard disk spec sheets. Using the information provided earlier, you can roughly esti-mate how many audio tracks the disk—in conjunction with your hard disk controller—can play back.

Av (Audio/Video) disks come highly recommended. These are tailored to audio and video applications and conse-quently support a relatively wide, continuous data stream.

Memory Capacity

If your bag is pop, rock or any of the new electronica styles, you will presumably need true audio tracks for vocals and solo instruments only; usually relatively short samples will take care of the rest. Some 300 MB per song should suffice.

You need an audio hard disk with at least **three gigabyte** to be able to work with four to five songs without a great deal of hassle when you switch from one song to another.

A 4 to 6 GB disk is advisable if you're planning on working with a fair old number of tracks and epic-length songs. If you go the whole hog and invest in a disk with nine gigabyte or higher, you are entering the professional realm. In this case, you certainly won't have any problems dealing with the com-ing 20 and 24-bit recording system generations.

As a rule—the higher the storage capacity of disks, the faster the throughput. Smaller hard disks are fragmented much more quickly, which means the maintenance intervals are shorter and the performance of the disk is degraded faster.

Installing Hard Disks

Whether you decide to install an audio disk in your computer or an external chassis is entirely up to you. An external housing is more versatile, but don't forget that there is a maximum allowable cable length for the Scsi bus which your setup may not exceed (see ›Cable Length‹ on page 40).

If you own a Macintosh with two Scsi busses, your choice should be clear. In this case, the internal Scsi interface is exactly twice as fast as the external interface. If you have a fast enough audio disk, installing it internally will give you twice the number of audio playback tracks.

There are a couple of factors you have to consider when you install any Scsi drive in a Macintosh: All current hard disks have the form factor (i. e. a standardized width) of 3.5" and can be installed in a 3.5" slot or, with an adapter rail, in a 5.25" slot. In desktop Macintoshes, you can generally install just one additional hard disk; in tower housings, up to four; in some clone models as many as ten.

When you're installing an additional internal Scsi disk, you still have to ensure that the Scsi bus is terminated correctly. The highest-performance drives have a tendency to generate a fair amount of heat, so you may need to install a more powerful internal fan.

Before you buy any Scsi disk that you want to install (or have someone install for you), you should check out it's overall height. Hard disks with small to medium capacities (up to nine gigabyte) generally have a height of 25.4 mm (1"), whereas larger disks require some 41 mm (1.6") or even more clearance. The former will always fit, the latter varies from model to model.

Magnetic Removable Media

Your choices aren't limited to hard disks. Contemporary removable disks give good performance, definitely good enough to use them for recording audio data. The nice thing about these is that once you've packed the medium full of data, all you have to do is pop in another—just like a diskette.

Even if you plan on recording audio data directly to a removable medium, you nevertheless need as high a data throughput as possible. Magneto-optical drives are relatively slow, they are only suitable if you are working with relatively

Removable cartridge media are very fast, but unfortunately not absolutely dependable. To protect against potential data loss, re-format magnetic media every couple of months and make a habit of generating backup copies.

few audio playback tracks (see ›Magneto-optical Removable Media‹ on page 43). Magnetic removables are substantially better—the newer types deliver nearly the speed of hard disks.

A wide range of products are available—if I listed them all, we would both be bored beyond all human endurance. Here's three recommended solutions for every wallet size:

◆ **Syquest Sparq:** The bottom line is that this removable comes cheap and gives max bang for your buck. A Fast Scsi version is in the works. These media have a capacity of some 900 Mb. The drawback—Syquest has yet to make any clear statements about minimum data throughput.

◆ **Iomega Jaz 1 Gb:** The 1-Gb Jaz drive is now considered a standard. The mean data throughput of the Fast Scsi drives is around 3.5 Mb/s.

Reasonably, the 2-Gb Jaz drive is compatible with 1-Gb Jaz media. In other words, you can read and write these in the bigger drive. However, the latter is not really a viable option because the smaller media slow the 2-Gb Jaz drive down to a point where it writes slower than its 1-Gb predecessor.

◆ **Iomega Jaz 2 Gb:** Inexplicably, none of Iomega's competitors were able to come up with anything that would give the 1-Gb Jaz a good run for its money, so the company went ahead and introduced its own rival—the 2-Gb drive. In addition to featuring double the capacity, the new kid on the block is also faster: Although the write speed of the Ultra Scsi drive is roughly equivalent to that of the 1-Gb version, at 6 Mb/s, its mean read throughput is nearly twice as high.

▶ If at some point the throughput of your Scsi disk causes you headaches, you can always buy another disk or two and have different disks and media play back different tracks, provided of course, your hard disk controller can deliver the goods.

The Scsi System

In a Scsi system with an 8-bit bus (Standard, Fast, Ultra), you can't connect more than eight Scsi devices. With a true 16-bit Scsi System (Wide, Ultra Wide, Ultra 2), the number of possible devices is doubled to 16. One of these devices is always the ›Master.‹ Usually the master is the computer with Scsi controller; it addresses the remainder of the Scsi devices.

The devices are connected to the Scsi bus in series, although communication between devices is executed in parallel. The computer is equipped with an external Scsi port which is connected to the first Scsi device in the chain. In models with two Scsi interfaces featured, one is an internal Scsi interface. Each Scsi device (excepting the master) is normally equipped with two Scsi ports. The purpose of the extra Scsi port is to daisy-chain the devices, i. e. it lets you connect another device to the previous device in the chain. There are a few other essential facts about Scsi systems that you should be familiar with:

Scsi Id

To ensure the controller addresses each Scsi device individually, you have to assign a unique or different identification number (Id) to each device in the Scsi chain. The standard procedure is to set jumpers (small switches) on the external Scsi device/s. The Macintosh—or more accurately its Scsi controller—is the master, which is always assigned Id 7, so don't give this Id to any other device. The internal program Scsi disk has the Scsi Id 0, an internal Scsi Cd-Rom drive Id 3. If you expand your setup with other Scsi devices, do not assign these reserved Ids to any other device. For that matter, it's essential that you assign each device a different number—if you make the mistake of giving two different devices identical numbers, chaos and confusion will rule.

▶ In Macintosh models with external Standard and internal Fast Scsi interfaces, the two busses operate completely independently. In this case you can assign the same Scsi Id number once internally and once externally.

Cable Length

Here's a general rule for Scsi systems: Every meter of cable adds to the error potential. Keep all cable connections as short as possible!

The cable length for a Scsi system may not exceed a total of six meters; the maximum cable length for a Wide Scsi bus is only three meters. Ultra 2 Scsi is a bit more generous, it will let you use twelve meters of cable. Keep in mind that when dealing with external devices, the length of an internal circuit from a device's Scsi port to the drive or board counts when you're tallying up total distance.

Cable Quality

If faults crop up in your Scsi system that can't be fixed by changing the Scsi Ids and termination, check out the cables and, if necessary, connect high-quality replacements (>Premium Quality<). If flat conductor cables are routed between Scsi devices in your setup, you'll find that higher quality cables will take care of a lot of headaches. Many people tend to focus on termination and configuration errors and underestimate the significance of cables as an error source.

Termination

Before you reconfigure the Scsi cable or termination setup, make absolutely certain that all (!) devices in the chain are switched off. If you don't, you may destroy essential, not to mention expensive, components or even entire Scsi devices.

In any Scsi system, the first and last device in the chain have to be equipped with a terminating resistor, a descriptively-named >terminator.< Sometimes you can activate this component via a software switch, but more often than not you'll have to set jumpers on the Scsi device.

The internal terminator in external Scsi devices is frequently switched off; in this case, you'll have to plug an external terminator into the unoccupied Scsi port. Choose an active terminator for this purpose, which is easy to identify because it is equipped with an integrated Led. An active terminator can execute corrective actions, which for just a few dollars (or your local equivalent) more, leads to more reliable performance of the entire Scsi bus.

▶ If the system is lacking a terminator, you may encounter data transmission errors and possibly Scsi system crashes. The same holds true if you make the mistake of doubling terminators up. If you're unsure, check out the system's behavior with and without an external terminator.

Connectors

Depending on the Scsi variant, different connector and port formats are used. For example, the external Macintosh Standard Scsi interface is a 25-pin connector, the internal Fast Scsi interface a 50-pin connector. Due to the fact that they are equipped with twice the number of circuits, Wide Scsi interfaces require 68-pin Scsi connectors.

You are free to connect Scsi devices featuring different standards to each other. You may need adapters, which your local computer shop will be more than happy to sell to you.

Prepping Audio Media

Regardless of whether you want to record audio data to a hard disk or directly to a removable medium, there are two things you have to keep in mind before you start formatting:

For optimum Vst performance, you should install an ›asynchronous hard disk driver.‹ Apple's own Hd Utility ›Drive Setup‹ supports this function and is now able to identify the majority of third-party vendors' drives.

If you use some other type of Hd formatting software, ensure that its ›Blind Transfers‹ option is activated. Otherwise data throughput will be insufficient and the degraded performance will lead to errors during audio playback.

You should avoid using Apple's new file system Hfs+, first introduced in the Mac Os 8.1, at least for your audio drives. For one, it's advantages are negligible when you're working with relatively large audio files. For the other, Vst—like many other programs that are optimized for high data throughput—is incompatible with Hfs+. Always format audio hard disks in the standard Hfs format.

Watch out, here comes that dreaded term again: Theoretically, you can connect Scsi devices with divergent specifications as you see fit. In practice, you may run into problems—for instance when you operate Narrow and Wide Scsi devices simultaneously on the same bus. In this type of scenario, make sure that the last Scsi device in the chain is a Wide device equipped with the appropriate termination.

▶ The standard software ›Hard Disk Toolkit‹ (HDT) by FWB is a comfortable alternative to Apple's formatting program ›Drive Setup‹ The software bearing the extension ›PE‹ is a light version. Although you will have to settle for relatively lean functions, it is mean enough for many users. HDT PE often comes as a freebie OEM version with new hard disks. When in doubt, bend your dealer's ear about it.

Maintaining Audio Media

The Macintosh file systems HFS and HFS+ are designed to spread the files across the hard disk's surface as uniformly or evenly as possible. Although this extends the life of the hard disks, it also tends to promote ›fragmentation,‹ a process in which files are chopped up into tiny tidbits of data.

The performance of highly fragmented disks suffers considerably; they also tend to wear out faster. Practice good ›audio disk maintenance‹ regularly, especially with smaller disks in the one to two gigabyte range, which should be defragmented at least once a month via suitable software.

You should also format your audio disk every two to three months—make sure you select the option ›Low-Level-Formatting.‹

▶ Your best bet for defragmenting hard disks are special software tools such as FWB's HDT mentioned above, or Symantec's Norton Utilities.

Data Backup

A lot of recording enthusiasts seem to enjoy flirting with disaster: They record audio tracks and hope for fortune to smile on the song until it's in the can, fully mastered. If the Kamikaze approach isn't your style, you should choose one of the following backup principles for your Vsт system, and stick to it with a missionaries zeal.

Dᴀᴛ Recorders

Vsᴛ Macintosh Version 3.5 and higher features an integrated Dᴀᴛ backup function. If you own a Macintosh audio card and an audio Dᴀᴛ recorder with digital interfaces, you can dump Vsᴛ audio data as complete data packets to Dᴀᴛ tapes, archive them and load them back at a later date.

However, audio Dᴀᴛ tape is not the best backup medium the world has ever seen: It's slow, relatively unwieldy and not a model of reliability. If you don't have any other backup option, by all means, use the Vsᴛ Dᴀᴛ backup function. It's definitely better than driving without this digital safety belt. If however, you are a relatively prolific home recorder and want to archive your creations safely for your grandchildren to enjoy, choose one of the following options.

Streamers

Streamers also store digital data on tape, but these devices and media were designed specifically for saving data, so this backup option beats Dᴀᴛ audio tapes hand down. For example, all streamers feature a control function where data is read during the write process by a second head and compared with the original data. A separate Verify routine is unnecessary.

There are diverse up-to-date streamer formats and concepts (e. g. Dᴅs4, Dʟᴛ, Qɪᴄ, Aɪᴛ) available. The differences among these lie in the respective recording techniques, tape materials and tape capacity (approx. 4 to 25 Gʙ).

Streamers are the most professional backup solution, but as usual, also the most expensive. This solution is feasible only if you use Vsᴛ to earn your daily bread and have to archive huge amounts of data on a regular basis.

Magneto-optical Removable Media

The fast magnetic removable media mentioned earlier are, at best, suitable for mid-term data backup. In the long run,

In the audio realm, the most widely used streamer format is ›Exabyte Tape.‹ Although the term is generally considered synonymous with 8-mm tapes, this is strictly speaking untrue—Exabyte is actually just the leading manufacturer of this species of streamers. ›Exabyte Tape‹ was for some time the sole standard medium—if you delivered anything other than this kind of medium to a Cᴅ mastering or pressing facility, you were laughed off the premises. Although it is still a common medium today, it looks as if Cᴅ-R masters will win out in the end.

you'll be better served with magneto-optical media—Mos for short—because these are substantially more reliable and more resistant to environmental influences.

Obviously, you need loads of capacity for any kind of reasonable audio data storage system. Currently, at 650 MB to 5.2 GB, only the 5.25" Mo drive will do. The latest generation of 5.2-GB Mo drives deliver data read throughput of some 3 MB/s and are thus suitable for direct audio data recording, provided you don't need the maximum possible number of parallel playback tracks.

The downside is that, here too, the drives and media are relatively pricey. We're not talking the second-mortgage-on-your-house level of the streamers, but you could definitely class this option in the ›professional‹ category.

We recommend the 5.25" Mo drives by Olympus and Sony, not because we own stock in the companies, but because they're well-established and widely used.

CD-R Recorders

Nowadays, drives as well as CD-R disks won't cost you an arm or a leg—for just a few bucks a pop, the disks are especially cheap considering that you get 650 MB of CD capacity. These handy little devices let you burn your own audio CDs, use CDs as audio data backups, and you have the added bonus of an extra CD-ROM drive in your setup. Ensure you choose a CD-R drive that features both ›Track at Once‹ and ›Disk at Once‹ modes. The latter is essential for burning audio CDs.

Currently, CD-RW burners for rewritable media (RW = ReWritable) aren't a worthwhile investment because the media are still ten times as expensive as CD-R's. Besides, CD-RW's can only be read by CD-RW burners and late-model CD-ROM drives, but not by audio CD players.

▶ When you're saving data, always activate the Verify function—it compares the original with the backup before you delete the original from a hard disk. The majority of programs execute the Verify routine automatically. A small scratch on a CD-R is enough to send a vocal track up in a puff of virtual smoke, and you don't stand a chance of retrieving it either. It's a good idea to make a backup of your backup for performances that can't be recaptured. Although it may seem like a hassle, you can't be too careful. Even if all of your double-jeopardy backup efforts save just one great vocal track, your effort will have paid off.

Monitors and Graphics Cards

For DTP applications, system vendors treat graphics systems with a priority usually reserved for royalty, whereas for audio applications, the graphics system is often considered nothing more than an afterthought. This is inconsiderate towards soon-to-be studio moles, because the quality of these components is decisive in determining how quickly, comfortably and efficiently you can work with your setup.

Monitors

Steinberg's express prerequisite for VST Macintosh operation is a graphical display featuring 256 colors and 832 × 624 pixels, which is the ›standard‹ 15" monitor setting. A monitor of this size is often part of a bargain-bin, all-in-one package. Do yourself a favor and pass on the offer—the monitor won't be able to simultaneously display all of the graphical elements that you need. Currently, you'll get the best mileage and VST performance with **17", 19" or 20" monitors**.

Don't make the mistake of concentrating solely on the diagonal measurement of the monitor. More important than a desktop aircraft carrier is a resolution that makes the stuff on the screen easily legible. Without going overboard, the recommended specs are resolutions of **1,024 × 768 pixels** (max. for 17"), **1,152 × 870 pixels** (max. for 19") and **1,280 × 960 pixels** (max. for 20").

Refuse to settle for any monitor that doesn't have a refresh frequency of at **least 75 Hz** and complies with the **Tco-95** norm. The former will protect your eyes, the latter your general health. A low-radiation monitor has another advantage: Your recording equipment won't be subjected to loads of electromagnetic interference, so you'll find there will be less stray hiss, hum and other peripheral noise in your audio signals.

Make your computer dealer work for his/her slice of the pie. Have him/her demonstrate different models with different resolutions, if at all possible, using your graphics card. Never buy a monitor by mail order unless you get a full refund-on-return warranty. Before you flash your cash, see if you can't talk the sales person into demonstrating the physical monitor you plan on taking home. Even with the same models of a series, there are often huge differences between ›on the shop floor‹ and ›out the back in a box‹ units.

▶ Not only are the compact dimensions and look of liquid crystal (Lc) monitors cool, they also have the advantage of producing virtually no electromagnetic interference, which is great for the studio. LC monitors are relatively expensive, but the price is bound to drop dramatically in the near future. When you're comparing prices, keep in mind that the amount of visible screen area on a 15" LC monitor is equivalent to that of a conventional 17" cathode ray monitor.

Every Windows PC multisync monitor can be used for the Macintosh. If the Macintosh control panel does not feature the resolution that a given monitor is able to produce, then the problem is generally due to the monitor cable or adapter. Apple has the solution—the universal Macintosh adapter. Third-party vendors also offer universal adapters that feature integrated mini-switches for adapting your setup to the monitor.

If you aren't planning on using your computer for professional-quality graphics and layout applications, you can make do with a compromise in true color and screen symmetry to keep a lid on your expenses.

Graphics Cards

Every Macintosh ships with at least one internal graphics card. If you want to boost the performance of your computer, a higher-quality card will sometimes do the trick. Although the enhanced color depth that this type of card delivers is not a big deal for VST operation, there are two possible improvements that may benefit VST users:

◆ Picture quality does not depend solely on the monitor; the graphics card also has a major influence. If you now own a hi-fi monitor and a lo-fi graphics card, a higher-quality graphics card could conceivably give you both a better resolution and refresh rate.

◆ A quality graphics card will considerably expedite picture setup. When you consider that, from Version 4.0, VST features switchable window configurations, this is an option definitely worth exploring.

In some computers (e. g. 7000 and 8000 series Power Macintoshes), you have the option of boosting the internal graphics card's performance by expanding the video RAM. Today, no less than 2 MB of graphics memory will do. **4 MB** is a good place to hang your hat; with a new graphics card, don't mess around with anything less.

Look, They're Twins (Two Monitors in Parallel)

Microsoft has been beating the drum about Windows 98's innovative capability of running two separate monitors in parallel, totally unaware (yeah, right) of the fact that the Macintosh operating system has offered this option for years. For a neat but weird trick if you've never tried it, you can use both screens as one, dragging objects from one screen to the next.

This is a handy little bit of technological magic for audio sequencers such as Vsт. In your Vsт window sets, you can define a larger monitor as your main working interface (e. g. for the Arrange window and Audio Mixer) and a smaller monitor for peripheral stuff such as Editors, Audio Performance Display or the Transport Bar. In addition to a second monitor, you'll also need a second graphics card—if it isn't (as in some Av Macintoshes) already installed.

The Ideal Vsт Macintosh

Now that you know all about what influence the key computer components and expansions have on your setup, here's a few bottom-line tips on buying a Vsт computer.

Original or Clone?

In the past few years, Apple has pursued a less xenophobic production policy of licensing their innovations to third-party vendors. These companies build and sell Macintosh-compatible computers—so-called ›clones.‹

Clones feature the same processors as original Apple computers. The motherboards are identical or slightly modified—usually the products of a joint effort by the clone maker and Apple. The big differences between the original and forgery are external factors such as the design of the housing and number of slots.

Throughout the remaining chapters in this book, I'll primarily stick to referring to the original Apple computers. Snobbery has nothing to do with it—there are simply too many clones available that a book of this scope could do justice to.

▶ The leading makers and resellers of Macintosh-compatible computers are Power Computing, Umax, Motorola, Daystar and Powertools.

▶ There's nothing to be said against investing in a Macintosh clone. On the contrary, these usually feature better expansion options, e.g. more PCI slots. The clone makers—under pressure from Apple—are in the process of a market draw-down, so before you fork over the dough for a Macintosh clone, find out exactly how long the manufacturer warrants or will continue to service the device.

Rejuvenating Old Macintoshes

It wasn't too long ago that even opening a Macintosh housing was considered a cardinal sin in the Macintosh world: ›Hardware handicrafts‹ were the sole domain of Windows PC users.

Those days are long gone. Nowadays when you ask a salesman about an upgrade card for Macintosh computers, be prepared for a lengthy speech. A ›real‹ computer upgrade focuses on the two key factors in computing performance—the clock and CPU type:

When you're contemplating the upgrading of your box, bear in mind you may be forced to also replace the Level 2 Cache to cater to the new and improved clock rate. With the G3 processor card, the Level 2 Cache is always accessed after the faster Backside Cache on the processor board. In this case, you should upgrade the Level 2 Cache to match the doubled performance of the Backside Cache, otherwise the former will slow the latter down.

◆ Clock: Many upgrade kits are designed to boost the CPU frequency by replacing the crystal-controlled oscillator or similar adventurous measures. This alone won't beef up performance by a considerable margin. The upper limit of a given clock enhancement also varies from computer to computer.

▶ The system bus clock follows the CPU clock in whole or half-step ratios (e. g. 1:2 or 1:3.5). Because the upper limit determined by the mainboard (in Power Macintoshes, 50MHz) may not be exceeded, a higher CPU clock rate may, under certain conditions, require a different ratio and thus a lower system bus clock rate. This is why, for example, a 233-MHz card may deliver poorer overall performance than a 200-MHz card.

◆ CPU: The plug-in CPU card is replaced in it's entirety with a current processor card. This is standard procedure for increasing the Cpu frequency and delivers a much greater boost in performance.

Method 1 is best left to ambitious computer Dıy nuts—I wouldn't recommend this type of home electronics experimentation. Method 2 is the way to go if your computer is ready for this kind of upgrade. For those experiencing budgetary woes, a second-hand Pcı Macintosh with a slot for a processor card might get the ball rolling until your horse finally finishes first.

▶ For a cost-effective processor upgrade, you should take a look at the so-called Mach-5 cards that several third-party vendors offer. Their price tag is usually well below the dearer G3 cards, but they do a good job of floating point computing, which translates to virtually the same level of Vsт performance as a comparable Apple brand-name card.

Can You Use a Powerbook as a Portable Studio?

For many of us, a fully-equipped computer studio that you can tote around with you seems a promising prospect indeed. So what's the deal, is it possible to run Vsт on a Powerbook and use it effectively as a port-a-studio?

At least two considerations put a damper on any hopes of using Windows compatible notebooks and portable Macintoshes, named ›Powerbooks,‹ as port-a-studios:

◆ In Powerbooks, all components are designed to consume as little power as possible, and the integrated hard disks are—comparatively speaking—as slow as frozen molasses. The boards usually run on a lower voltage, which may also lead to audio processing problems.

◆ Contemporary portable computers do not feature standard Pcı slots so you can't install the type of audio card that you need for this application.

In contrast to Windows Pcs, all Macintosh models released over the past few years feature a standardized 16-bit sound system on board, which means that you can only operate a Powerbook with Apple's own audio hardware (Av mode).

To be honest, the audio quality is pretty unsatisfying—if you give it a try, other descriptive terms may come to mind. You could conceivably execute ›administrative‹ tasks such as arrangement, cutting and audio editing on a Powerbook, but as far as recording audio goes, you should consider it more of a sophisticated ›dict-a-phone,‹ useful for making a ›rough sketch‹ of a spur-of-the-moment idea.

If you are planning on buying a Powerbook as a portable demo studio or a handy post-editing tool, some advice before you reach for your credit card:

If a Wallstreet series Powerbook has caught your eye as a potential VST computer, go for a model with 250 MHz clock or higher. The Wallstreet/233 models do without the Level 2 Backside Cache, which VST in turn, can't do without. An upgrade is out of the question.

◆ According to Steinberg, only the Powerbook 2400, 3400 and G3 series are VST-tested and approved. The official word isn't out yet on the 1400 series. Older Powerbooks are not supported in full because Apple left a couple of key components out of the package. If you own one of these, you will have to settle for a VST performance equivalent to—at the most—three to four audio playback tracks.

◆ If you want to travel in style, the current G3 Powerbooks of the Wallstreet series are pretty impressive. Your cash flow allowing, these little monsters actually give you a portable VST studio, which—bar the quality of audio recording—can more than match the performance of high-end desktop models. The current flagship model features 292 MHz and a 400 MHz version is in the works—optimists say the sky's the limit.

Performance Limits

Now that you know what components are suitable for your VST system, you may wonder what you can expect from the hardware in terms of performance.

Cᴘᴜ Type	Cᴘᴜ Clock	RAM	Performance
Pᴘᴄ-603	180 MHz	32 Mʙ	20 audio tracks with one LQ-EQ each, 2 standard plug-ins
Pᴘᴄ-604e	200 MHz	32 Mʙ	24 audio tracks with a total of 32 LQ-EQs, 5 standard plug-ins
Pᴘᴄ-750 (G3)	300 MHz	64 Mʙ	32 audio tracks with EQs (HQ and LQ mixed), 10 standard plug-ins

You'll find a number of examples in the table to the left. You should however consider these more a rough ›guesstimate‹ than the law according to Wɪᴢoo. ›LQ-EQ‹ stands for the internal Low-Quality EQ bands, ›HQ-EQ‹ for the deluxe version which requires approx. seven times the Cᴘᴜ power.

As you can gather, Vsт delivers pretty impressive results on a computer that just barely satisfies Steinberg's minimum requirements. This hints at a concept you may have already pondered—the program will run on slower computers. Although you will soon find yourself pushing the limits in terms of Eǫs and plug-ins, owners of an older box may settle for this compromise until the time is right for an upgrade.

Even extremely fast computers peak out at 32 audio tracks. Although the computer might have some kick left in it, even the fastest of audio hard disks can't hack the pace. In all honesty though, this limit—which you can circumvent somewhat via Track Bouncing—is almost irrelevant for the vast majority of applications.

What is extremely relevant, however, is the number of Eǫs and effects you can play with at the same time—you'll find there never seems to be enough of these to go around. A mid-class Macintosh with a 604e Cᴘᴜ has enough in reserve for standard mixdowns with the usual effects condiments and won't start sweating it until you begin using some of the plug-ins by third-party vendors. These little piranhas see a Cᴘᴜ and start a feeding frenzy—just two of them can devour everything your Cᴘᴜ has to offer.

So, if you're a big fan of the highest quality plug-ins and Eǫs known to man, you have no choice but to shell out the bucks for a powerful G3 model. With the current G3 Macintosh and requisite peripheral stuff, you'll be able to really enjoy VST without having to worry about running out of juice for the EQs and VST plug-ins, and still have enough power left over for two high-class reverb plug-ins such as the Waves ›TrueVerb.‹

Tops & Flops

To close out the chapter on computer hardware, we'll first take a look at the Macintosh models that we rate highly, and then some that don't make the grade. This ›VST Richter scale‹ should give you a helping hand in classing and rating models that aren't listed.

Recommendations

All of the listed computers work with two SCSI busses—they feature an internal Fast SCSI bus. The exceptions are the Apple G3 models that are equipped with two internal E-IDE interfaces—they feature the slow Standard SCSI bus only.

If you are in the market for a new VST computer, buy it only if it fulfills the following three criteria:

◆ CPU on a plug-in card
◆ Level 2, Inline or Backside Cache
◆ At least three PCI slots

Virtually all current and many older Macintosh models meet our standards, e. g.:

◆ PM 7500 (PPC-601, 3 × PCI, 2 × SCSI)
◆ PM 7600 (PPC-604, 3 × PCI, 2 × SCSI)
◆ PM 8500 (PPC-604, 3 × PCI, 2 × SCSI)
◆ PM 7300 (PPC-604e, 3 × PCI, 2 × SCSI)
◆ PM 8600 (PPC-604e, 3 × PCI, 2 × SCSI)

If you are planning to set up a top-notch VST system that meets the most discerning demands, you'll find that three PCI slots just don't cut it. In this case, we recommend the—unfortunately expensive—models with six PCI slots, such as:

◆ PM 9500 (PPC-604, 6 × PCI, 2 × SCSI)
◆ PM 9600 (PPC-604e, 6 × PCI, 2 × SCSI)

For the highest computing power without resorting to processor upgrades, the G3 models are the only way to go. The conundrum is that in this category of computers, Apple doesn't offer anything with more than three Pci slots. So, if you think that you'll need loads of slots, you'll have to check out the clone market. As discussed earlier, the licenses for these brands are about to run out, but my educated guess is that these companies stock will last until at least the end of '98.

▶ In the appendix (page 169), you'll find a bunch of Internet links to Macintosh hardware archives. There, some kind souls went to the trouble of compiling exhaustive lists of all Macintoshes ever built by Apple and clone makers, along with their specifications. If you're looking at buying a second-hand box, these archives are a great help.

Caution—Hands Off

Unfortunately, there are a bunch of computers that you should avoid buying for diverse reasons:

Nubus: Buy this type of computer only if you are absolutely convinced that you will never need a current audio card for Vsт and the computer is a steal.

Hard-wired Cpu: You can't boost processor performance by plugging in a new Cpu.

Pм 4400: The Power Macintosh 4400, as well as the many clones based on the same board design (›Tanzania‹), are the computer equivalent of New Coca-Cola—a failure of staggering proportions. Aside from the soldered Cpu, these boxes pose other serious problems: There are wild deviations in the components (e. g. Raм and Dмa chips). What this means is that astoundingly a Pм 4400 *may* work with Vsт, but in all likelihood *won't*. If a smiling person offers you one, run.

All-in-ones: The new ›Artemis‹ might be a great movie screen for hamsters, but you won't have any fun with it. Evidently Europe will be spared—›Artemis‹ won't be released there. Although it and the ›iMac‹ offer G3 processors at a low price, the expansion options are—well, there simply aren't

Apparently the number 4 is considered a symbol of death in many Asian countries, so the Pм 4400 went over like a lead balloon. It ended up being re-named Pм 7220 and unloaded fire-sale style. Sometimes superstition is the writing on the wall: The Pм 4400, or whatever code name it goes by in your neighborhood, is a dud in terms of Vsт—avoid it all costs!

any. The 15" monitor is too small to be practical, and don't bother looking for any Pcɪ slots, you won't find 'em. The ›iMac‹ boldly goes where no computer has gone before—it doesn't feature a floppy disk drive and, rather than an Scsɪ interface, it features the universal but sadly slow Universal Serial Bus (Usʙ)—so forget about connecting another hard disk.

These computers may be fine for what they were designed for—handy little Internet toys, 21st century fishbowls or the like, but they don't cut it for Vsт.

3 The Sound System

Vsт's internal audio system works with 32-bit resolution. In principle, this gives you a dynamic range of up to 144 dB, which is plenty for even the most demanding tastes.

Depending on the computer's audio system, these capabilities are exploited anywhere from barely scratching the surface to delivering the whole hog. However, before we get ahead of ourselves and start selecting audio hardware, we'll take a look at how the components work in conjunction with Vsт.

Asio Drivers

Asio (**A**udio **S**tream **I**nput **O**utput) drivers interface between the software (Vsт) and hardware (internal Macintosh audio system or audio card). In essence, an Asio driver is a modular software interface via which audio data is transported to Vsт from the sound system (recording) and from Vsт to the sound system (playback).

The ASIO Drivers Folder

Vsт ships with a number of Asio drivers which are located in the Asio Drivers folder in the Vsт Program folder. Each of these Asio drivers has the task of linking specific audio hardware to Vsт. A driver name will tell you exactly what make and model of hardware this is, e. g. Asio Korg 1212.

If you're thinking about using audio hardware for which a driver is not included with Vsт, you will need to get the appropriate Asio driver from the manufacturer of the hardware and copy the file to the Asio Drivers folder.

▶ When you're shopping for an audio card, be sure to select a model for which Macintosh Asio drivers exist. Only then will you be able to fully enjoy the capabilities of the card and computer.

When Vst is first booted, it checks out the Asio drivers in the Asio Drivers folder and loads files relevant to your hardware, ready for any additional setup necessary in the selection dialogs.

▶ Theoretically (there's that word again), you could leave all of the Asio drivers that you don't need in the Asio Drivers folder. In my experience however, these are a common source of errors. After you have set up the system to your satisfaction, you should cut all Asio drivers that you don't need and paste them somewhere else. Any folder that Vst doesn't scan will do.

The driver files for the active audio hardware must be located in the Asio Drivers folder. Park all other Asio drivers that you don't need in a ›neutral‹ folder. You can name the folder whatever you like; in this example we unimaginatively used (ASIO).

Activating Asio Drivers

In the audio system, you can select the driver for your card from the pop-up-menu Asio Device and activate it permanently.

Go to the Options menu under Audio Setup and select the menu item System.

Click on the Launch Field to open a box listing hardware-specific parameters. This type of box usually includes stuff like the input level, monitor mode and the input switching function for audio hardware devices if these can't be run in parallel. If this type of audio hardware control menu actually exists, any functions featured will depend on the software that ships with the particular audio hardware. Vst does nothing more than retrieve and open this specific control panel—provided, of course, that it does indeed exist.

In most cases, you won't have to worry about any of the other parameters. VST sets the ›Expert Parameters‹ automatically to match the selected audio card type. Change these parameters only when you run into problems and you know exactly what you're doing when you attempt to fix them.

What Is Latency and What Does It Mean to Me?

In the VST Audio System Setup, the selection menu for the ASIO drivers features a field that contains a tidbit of vital information. You can't enter anything here; the program uses it to give you a key stat called ›latency.‹ This is much the same as what your first period teacher once berated you about—tardiness. It describes the time it takes for VST and the audio hardware to route a signal from the audio input to the output. This can be an appreciable delay.

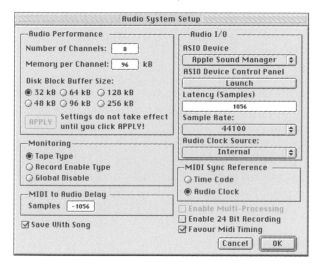

Activate the ASIO driver in the VST Audio System Setup. The majority of other parameters are set automatically; you shouldn't change these unless you have a specific objective in mind.

Every digital audio system requires a number of computing cycles to execute audio manipulations. This means that latency is inherent in all digital audio hardware and software—including digital reverbs, digital mixers and effects plug-ins. So the question is not *if* latency exists but rather: ›How much latency are you dealing with?‹—or even more practically: ›Will the latency trash your recording?‹

Vst indicates latency in sample units. The value of the increments depends on the sampling rate. With the standard sampling rate of 44.1 kHz, we're talking about:

◆ Latency samples × (1,000 ms / 44,100 samples) = latency in milliseconds

Example: Latency = 1,056 Samples × (1,000 ms / 44,100 samples) = approx. 24 ms.

At this latency value, when you're monitoring an audio recording via your system, you will hear the Vst monitor signal 24 ms later than you are actually playing. With rhythmic instruments, a latency of this order will do a serious tap dance on your nerve endings.

Vst latency is influenced primarily by three factors:

◆ Operating system version

◆ Your computer's speed

◆ Audio hardware and Asio drivers

The most important factor is how well your computer does its job: The faster the computer, the lower the latency. The latency of an elderly Macintosh runs up to 1,056 samples (approx. 24 ms), whereas G3 models in Av mode equipped with Sound Manager drivers (see page 61) have a latency of just 512 samples (approx. 11.6 ms) and are thus within a tolerable range. There you go, yet another reason to plunder the piggy bank and invest in a fast G3 Macintosh for Vst.

A universal tolerance level for latency is impossible to define. It depends on the recording situation, audio material, rhythmic sensibility and possibly most significantly, personal taste and tolerance. For my part, tempers start flaring at anything over 10 to 12 milliseconds (approx. 500 samples).

Out-smarting Latency

If you record keyboards to Vst first as Midi tracks and later record the sound generators' output signals as audio signals, you will hear the audio recording signal lag behind the original Midi track—how much depends on your system. This brief delay is precisely equivalent to the current latency. By delaying the Midi signals in Vst by the same value, you can put the two signals back in sync:

1   Open the Audio System Setup menu and check out the Latency value of your system.

2   Enter the opposite value to the field labeled Midi To Audio Delay (left bottom)—at a latency of 1,024 samples this value would be ›–1024.‹ Don't forget to make it a negative value—add a minus symbol in front of the number!

3   Close the dialog box and check out the influence that this entry has on the audio recording of a Midi track when you play back and monitor them simultaneously.

Now the Midi and audio tracks in your system should run in absolute sync.

Av Audio without Additional Hardware

In contrast to Windows Pcs, which normally require an additional soundcard, all of the Macintosh models released over the past few years come complete with a 16-bit stereo audio system. If it's quality is enough to float your boat, you won't need an additional audio card to record and play back audio via Vst.

This ›stand-alone mode‹ without an additional audio card is called ›Av mode.‹

▶   ›Av‹ is a common acronym for ›Audio/Video,‹ which leads to all kinds of confusion: ›Av hard disks‹ are well-suited for video and audio applications because they feature continually high data throughput. ›Av Macintosh‹ computers on the other hand are generally nothing more than models with enhanced video features. In other words, you don't need an ›Av Macintosh‹ for Vst—all Apple computers that are suitable for Vst ship with an on-board 16-bit sound system.

How Does a Macintosh Sound?

Apple G3 computers equipped with the Av Personality card feature integrated audio hardware that sounds a heck of a lot better than the standard system. If you don't want to invest in an additional audio card, these models might do the trick for you.

Macintosh audio hardware is limited to a stereo input and output. It lets you record audio in the CD standard 16-bit/44.1 kHz digital format and generate CD masters directly.

This however applies to the technical format of the files only and not their audio quality. Personally, ›CD quality‹ is not the term that comes to mind when I'm pondering the stuff that the Macintosh audio hardware puts out. The usual undesirable side-effects that you have to contend with in budget audio cards are all rather prominent. The Macintosh audio system is just peachy keen for demo productions, but it certainly won't replace a professional audio card.

Optimizing Audio Quality

If you want to, or are forced to, work exclusively with the Macintosh audio hardware, don't despair, there are a few tricks that will improve the quality of your recordings:

◆ Although a microphone symbol often graces the stereo 1/8" input, never plug a microphone directly into this input unless your bag is serious lo-fi sound. Invest in a decent studio microphone and a suitable preamp. Patch a line signal from the preamp to your Macintosh.

◆ Even if your Macintosh model is equipped with additional RCA audio inputs, use the minijack instead because it has a signal-to-noise ratio that is some 6 dB higher, which means there will be less hiss in your recordings.

◆ Pre-mix signals that belong together anyway—e. g. stacked keyboard sounds—to make a single mono or stereo recording instead of recording each separately. The fewer recording operations that you can get by with, the less unwanted noise you'll end up with in your mix.

◆ Never record loops from audio sampling CDs analog—always import this audio data digitally via the CD-ROM drive of your computer. If at all possible, stick to special sampling CD-ROMs that let you import material directly in AIF format.

The Apple Sound Manager

The integrated 16-bit-audio hardware of a Macintosh requires a standardized software interface to allow programs such as VST to input and output audio. In the Mac Os, this is the system extension ›Sound Manager.‹

Instead of the rather Spartan ›Monitors and sound‹ control panel options, programs such as VST often feature their own dialog boxes in which you can define the input and output parameters.

DAV or Sound Manager Driver?

VST treats the Macintosh audio hardware, or more accurately its software representative the Sound Manager, like a normal audio card with stereo input and output. However, you can choose from two Asio drivers as an interface to the Macintosh sound system:

- **Apple DAV:** This driver's programming is very hardware-specific, which lightens the load on the computer and delivers better performance. However, as with any hardware-specific programming, you'll find that the DAV driver does not work perfectly for every combination of computer and Mac Os.

- **Apple Sound Manager:** The is the standard Asio driver for the Sound Manager. Although it is a bit more ›sluggish‹ than the DAV driver, it is compatible with all computer models. You would be hard-pressed to find a more reliable driver in terms of operating stability.

If you want to run your Macintosh in Av mode, try the Apple DAV driver first. Even if it runs like a dream, give it a trial period because it may cause weird stuff to happen in your computer such as ›crackling‹ noises or other irritating errors.

In this case, go for the Apple Sound Manager driver.

▶ I don't want to be wishy-washy, but it is difficult to make any blanket statements about which of the two drivers works best with which hardware/software combination. The Dav Asio driver that ships with Vst 4.0 generally runs well on Mac Os 7.x, Mac Os 8.1 and Mac Os 8.5, but not on Mac Os 8.0. The good news is that if one of the two drivers doesn't work, the other will. You'll just have to try them to find out for sure.

Sound Manager as an Audio Middleman

If Vst can't actually communicate with a particular piece of audio hardware and there is no appropriate Asio driver available, you do have an option, albeit a limited one: Most Macintosh-compatible audio cards let you interface them directly to the Sound Manager. What happens here is that the internal Macintosh sound system is disabled and the audio card's stereo input and outputs are used instead.

In a round-about manner, you can interface stereo I/O audio cards to Vst via the Sound Manager. However, there are a bunch of disadvantages to this type of setup; it should only be considered a temporary solution at best.

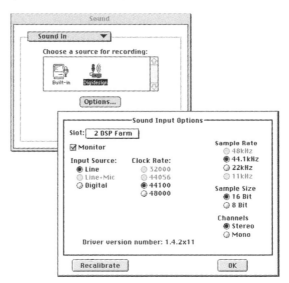

Now that you know how Vst addresses the Sound Manager, you've probably already guessed that you can use the latter as a middleman to communicate with audio cards for which you don't have a special Asio driver. Proceed as follows:

1 You will need a software driver for the audio card to link it to the Apple Sound Manager; it should have been included in the factory package. Copy this hardware-specific driver (for example Digidesign calls these Sound Drivers) to the Extensions folder in the Macintosh System folder.

2 Unfortunately, you can't select the new audio hardware directly in the control panel Monitors and Sound. You first have to install the control panel Sound, which you'll find on your Mac Os System Cd or on Apple's Internet support pages.

3 After you've installed the control panel and application, you can activate the alternative audio hardware. Depending on the hardware that you're dealing with, you may have other options available.

4 Now the audio hardware should be active in the Sound Manager. Check if the system's sounds are automatically routed through this hardware.

5 If the audio card indeed interfaces with the Sound Manager, all you have to is talk to it in the usual manner via Vst. For this purpose, in Vst activate the standard solution Apple Sound Manager as the Asio driver.

6 Now you should be able to address a stereo input and output of the audio card via Vst.

This type of Diy interface to audio hardware via the Sound Manager has diverse disadvantages, for instance:

♦ The setup is limited to one stereo input and output,

♦ 16-bit quality at the max, regardless of the hardware,

♦ and your computer has to carry a heavy load (latency, sluggish system response).

Use this method only if you already own an audio card for which an Asio driver is not yet available.

▶ When you go shopping for a new card, ignore models that do not come complete with a native Asio driver.

Currently, audio input and output via Sound Manager is limited to stereo only; a multi-channel format is proposed, but don't hold your breath while you're waiting for it to happen.

If a native ASIO driver is available for your card, smile. This guarantees the best possible direct interface that supports all physical audio inputs and outputs.

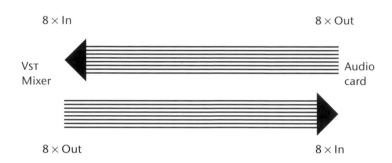

To interface an audio card via the Sound Manager, you will need the right driver for the audio card. Even then your audio system is limited to one stereo in/out and 16-bit quality at the max.

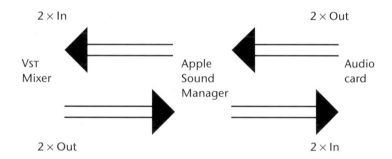

The Right Audio Card

Today, there is a good selection of audio cards for the Macintosh available. You can choose anything from simple stereo I/O cards through to modular multi-I/O interfaces with professional digital interfaces and converters.

Here are the most important terms that you'll come across in audio card product flyers and during the course the following chapters:

Duplex Mode

Just because a card comes complete with two or more inputs and outputs, it doesn't necessarily mean you can access these simultaneously. With so-called ›half-duplex‹ cards featuring two channels, you can only record audio after you have switched the audio output off and vice versa.

The implications of this limitation are significant: You can't listen to a previously recorded audio track while you're recording a new track—as you can well imagine, this won't have you jumping for joy with all the creative possibilities. Ensure that the audio card you end up buying supports ›full-duplex‹ mode. All of the cards recommended below provide unconditional support of full-duplex mode.

S/P-Dif I/O

I/O is short for input/output. S/P-Dif (**S**ony/**P**hilips-**D**igital **I**nter**F**ace) is the most common format for digital interfaces. Many audio cards feature an input and output in this format., It is worth noting that the S/P-Dif interface—as well as the professional quality Aes/Ebu interface—operate in stereo, despite only having a single connector in and a single connector out.

If you own a Dat recorder, you should go for a card featuring S/P-Dif I/O. It lets you transfer audio data back and forth between the Dat recorder and your computer without any signal degradation.

Some cards let you use the S/P-Dif I/O interface in parallel with other interfaces, although in practice this rarely gives you any advantages worth mentioning (see ›Digidesign Audiomedia 3‹ on page 68).

Other cards are limited solely to S/P-Dif I/O and do without analog audio interfaces altogether. Does this mean this type of card should be avoided at all costs?

Not necessarily: If you already own a good Dat recorder, you can most likely use it as an external Ada converter and thus attain the quality level of better audio cards. Before you go card shopping, check if your Dat recorder supports this option!

Adat and TDIF-I/O

Digital multi-channel interfaces used in conjunction with VST are on their way to becoming a staple in professional studio environments. Here eight digital signals—i. e. mono tracks—are transported simultaneously via a single cable. This capability is a pretty neat option to have when you are planning on using VST in combination with a digital multi-track recorder, and also comes in handy if you happen to own or have access to a digital hardware mixing console.

The Adat optical format enables signals with up to 24-bit word width, but currently the electronic components of the interface limit its capability to 20 bits at the maximum. An improved version is in the works. If you're looking at putting together a high-end 24-bit recording system, be sure to find out exactly what the limitations of the hardware's Adat interfaces are before you pay the man.

If you own a Tascam digital recorder, you should definitely go for an interface featuring TDIF (Tascam Digital InterFace). If you own, or are planning to buy equipment by other vendors, the Adat multi-channel interface by Alesis seems well on it's way to becoming an industry standard. It is actually an optical interface featuring a fiber-optic cable, which has a number of practical advantages, including the option of using much longer cables and greater resistance to electromagnetic interference.

With this type of interface, you can do without analog interfaces of any type. You can use the converter installed in the external digital recorder or mixing console and route exclusively digital signals to the computer—essentially the same procedure that you would use for a DAT recorder.

Audio Converters

Presumably one of the most important considerations for you will be the audio quality of your setup. The converters for the analog interfaces are an important criteria. For many years, 16-bit converters were the standard, but now a new generation of converters featuring 20 or even 24-bit word width is supplanting these components.

But don't be fooled: I'm willing to wager that all of your favorite CDs were recorded with 16-bit gear (maybe even analogue!). They still sound pretty good though, don't they? You should be taking a closer look at the other audio quality specs to see if they meet your personal standards. In this context, more bits doesn't necessarily equal better sound.

The current converter generation works with 18 or 20 bits. Besides, the potential of 24-bit recording and 96-kHz sampling won't be fully realized until new Cᴅ standards such as Dᴠᴅ (**D**igital **V**ersatile **D**isc with 24-Bit/96-kHz audio) have been established. You can cool your heels until at least the turn of the millennium while you're waiting for this to happen.

Internal/External

The card/converter setup in high-end audio systems is split: A card installed in the computer is connected to at least one external conversion unit via a special cable. The latter is often housed in a 19" chassis, along with the Aᴅᴀ converters and audio ports.

Not only is this type of setup easier to handle, the external box is usually equipped with a discrete power supply, which means the converter isn't exposed to high-frequency interference that typically runs rampant within a computer's housing. Unless you're into very industrial sounds, you'll certainly enjoy the enhanced sound quality.

Cascading

Many cards feature an option where you can use two or even more units in parallel. For instance, you could give your lonely stereo I/O card some company and drop in another identical card: Presto, you now have a 4-way I/O system. Again, before you part with any moolah, ensure the card and its drivers provide unconditional support for this type of option.

Drivers

Audio card vendors have discovered a fun new pastime: Announce a Vsᴛ Asɪᴏ driver is in the works and then never deliver on the promise. Hey, it moves units and it's free publicity.

Instead of wasting time on soothsayers, in the following section we'll stick to Macintosh-compatible audio cards for which VST ASIO drivers are available or at least in the hot little hands of the Steinberg testing team.

Stereo I/O Cards

When you're mentally gearing yourself up for your component shopping spree, you first have to figure out the prospective number of audio inputs and outputs—often abbreviated as I/O. It would be simple enough if less costly audio hardware featured fewer ins and outs and more expensive equipment more of the same, but this is not always the case.

Again, your choice hinges on the way you work: If you subscribe to the overdub recording method—i. e. one instrument after another—and plan on executing all audio editing and processing tasks on your computer, then a card featuring a single stereo input and output will do you just fine:

Digidesign Audiomedia 3

◆ PCI, 2 × Analog In, 2 × Analog Out, 18-bit converter, S/P-DIF In/Out, RCA audio jacks on the card's chassis.

This ASIO driver, developed jointly by Steinberg and Digidesign, is ready to roll. It supports 4-channel recording and 4-channel playback in Full-Duplex mode. Although the Audiomedia 3 is designed as a stereo I/O card, you can, with some reservations, use it as a 4-channel I/O system in VST Macintosh:

For 4-channel operation, you will have to address the stereo digital (S/P-DIF) and analog interface in parallel—both at the input and output ends. This option will only be of any practical benefit if you have a special hardware setup replete with additional stereo converters.

Lucid Technology PCI 24

◆ Pci, Digital Stereo I/O (as Aes/Ebu and S/P-Dif respectively), audio jack on the slot chassis; support of digital input signals with 8 to 48 kHz sampling rates with realtime sample rate conversion at 44.1 or 48 kHz; max. 20-bit In/ 24-bit Out, integrated Motorola 56301 Dsp to lighten the Cpu's load.

Here too, the Asio driver for Vst Macintosh is ready. The card is limited to stereo digital interfaces, so you can use these sensibly with the requisite digital equipment.

A 2-channel Ada converter would also do the trick. Lucidly, the company recognized this business opportunity and offers a suitable unit:

The Ada 1000 is a stereo analog/digital translator with 20-bit converters and fits the Pci 24 like a glove (and the Nubus version Nb 24 as well, see page 75). With this combination—Pci 24 and Ada 1000—you would end up with a high-quality stereo I/O system which supports both analog and digital signals at it's inputs and outputs.

Multi I/O Systems

This term is used to describe cards or systems that feature more than just the obligatory stereo input or output. Anything more than two inputs is a good idea if you occasionally want to record more than just a single stereo signal, for instance a complete acoustic drum set, a string quartet or even an entire band. Most users are satisfied with one stereo input but want more outs, so some companies make cards with eight or more outs.

When you use Vst in combination with one of these ›multi-out‹ cards, you have a de facto enhanced master section with oodles of individually variable master outs. At all important locations within the mixer's signal routing circuit (channel outputs, Fx sends and returns) you can route signals via these master ›busses‹ whenever you see fit. With this type of card, your VST mixer has ten physical outputs rather than the standard two.

Take a closer look at this species of card when you're planning on using the VST mixer in combination with an external multi-track recorder, mixing console and/or hardware effects processors.

When VST is used in conjunction with multi-out cards, next to patching external effects or filters into the mix, the setup offers even more sophisticated possibilities such as special headphones mixes for monitoring purposes.

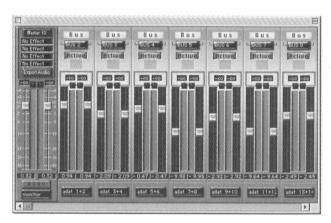

Korg 1212 I/O

◆ PCI, 2 × Analog I/O (20-bit A/D, 18-bit D/A Converters), S/P-DIF I/O, 8-channel Adat I/O, Adat Sync-In, Wordclock Sync.

◆ In VST, you can use all inputs and outputs simultaneously (a max. of 12-way I/O).

This card was a bit of a breakthrough—the first featuring a native ASIO driver for VST Macintosh. The ASIO interface, developed jointly by Korg and Steinberg, is very reliable and fast—low latency guaranteed. Another selling point are the high-quality converters used in this interface.

With only 2-way analog I/O but 10-way digital I/O, I can only recommend this card to users of Adat or Adat-compatible devices. However, because of its fair price and the aforementioned attributes, the card is a steal for this type of application.

▶ Many professional audio cards use Adat optical interfaces. With an external conversion unit, you can also connect these systems to analog gear. Two very good converter units are available from Creamware: A8 (1 × Adat I/O ⇔ 8-channel Analog I/O; recommended for the Korg 1212 I/O)
A16 (2 × Adat I/O ⇔ 16-channel Analog-I/O; recommended for the Sonorus StudI/O)

Sonorus StudI/O

◆ Pci, Analog Stereo Out, 2 × Optical I/O each. Each of these can be switched to S/P-Dif or 8-channel Adat format. In Vst, you can use a maximum of 16 ins and 18 outs per card simultaneously.

The concept is much like a ›double‹ Korg 1212 I/O, although you should be aware that it isn't equipped with an analog input. Here too, you'll need a direct connection to digital hardware (mixer/recorder) with Adat interfaces or an appropriate conversion unit (Creamware; see above).

The Macintosh Asio driver is not included in the Vst package, but it does ship with the card. You can also download it from the Sonorus homepage (see page 176). The driver was developed solely by Sonorus, but it's qualities are impressive enough to motivate Steinberg to recommend it unequivocally: You can define the bit width of the data stream directly, which means that data transport via the Pci bus can be adapted to the given requirements (16/20/24-bit recording).

The Asio parameter field lets you define the latency (see page 58) within the framework of the computer's performance capability. Theoretically, you can reduce it to 128 samples which is equivalent to a virtually inaudible delay of some three milliseconds. Although currently none of the Macintoshes can deliver this kind of performance, the point is that you can adapt the Asio driver perfectly to every level of computing performance.

There are several cards on the market featuring hardware that is identical to the Sonorus StudI/O. These include the Creamware T-Dat 16 and Prodif Platinum. According to Steinberg, these card makers do not currently offer Macintosh Asio drivers. This is why our official recommendation goes to the Sonorus StudI/O.

Another advantage of the StudI/O is particularly interesting for professional users: You can cascade up to three cards, which gives a you a system with a whopping 56 digital outs.

Multi I/O Systems with Dsp Effects

Increasingly, audio systems featuring internal Dsp computing power are hitting the market. What this means to you is that you have access to additional filters, compressors or multi-effects that are actually computed by the card. Vst remains unaffected. In other words, the program's user interface isn't slowed down by any measure. You can enjoy the use of just as many Vst Eqs and/or plug-ins as well as the add-on Dsp performance of the audio card!

On the downside, Vst is designed so that all of the requisite computing for audio processing is executed exclusively by the computer's Cpu. In practical terms, this means that Vst does support the Dsp capabilities of the card, but that these are not fully integrated in the mixer's user interface:

Yamaha Dsp Factory

◆ Basic Pci card Ds2416 with 2 × Analog I/O (20-Bit Converter) each and S/P-Dif-I/O.

◆ Among other features, the Dsp capacity comprises an internal digital mixer similar to the Yamaha 02R/03D with 10 Bus Outs, 6 Aux Sends, parametric 4-Band Eqs with a total of 104 frequency bands, 26 dynamic processors for compressors/gates, as well as 2 Rev500 multi-effects processors.

◆ The system manages up to eight input and sixteen output signals internally. With the appropriate expansions, you can access these circuits via physical audio interfaces. The Ax44 expansion for example offers 4 × Analog I/O each and a Headphones Out.

◆ Additional expansions featuring digital interfaces are in the works. Both the basic card and the interface expansions are cascadable, so you can upgrade the system to a maximum of 16 inputs and 32 outputs.

◆ At time of printing, the Asio drivers for this system weren't quite finished, but according to Steinberg/Yamaha, should be out any day now. In Vst, the internal DsP Factory software mixer will be represented by an additional mixer user interface, letting you work with it and the internal Vst mixer simultaneously. You will be able to flexibly route audio signals back and forth between the two software mixers.

▶ In the mid-class price range, Yamaha's DsP Factory is undoubtedly the most interesting sound system for VsT. When you're tallying up your budget, keep in mind that you will need the ›pro version‹ VsT/24 to integrate the DsP Factory. More on this topic in ›Which Cubase Version Is Best for You?‹ on page 18.

Currently, Yamaha's DsP Factory is the DsP card that will give you the biggest bang for your buck. A complete O2R digital mixer is integrated on the cascadable Pci card, which you can manipulate within VsT via an additional mixer user interface.

Lexicon Studio System

- Basic Pci card Core 32 (cascadable).

- Modular high-end system featuring a 24-Bit Digital Audio Bus and 24-Bit Converters.

- Expansion options up to 32 audio channels and 44 audio outputs. Diverse cascadable external 19" converter units are available. Among other features, Ldi-12T Stereo Analog I/O (20-Bit Converter), S/P-Dif I/O and 8-Channel Adat Optical I/O.

- The big daddy of modularly upgradable interfaces is called Ldi-16S. The basic version offers 8-Channel Analog I/O (balanced Xlr). The following expansions are planned: Aes-8 (8-Channel Aes/Ebu I/O incl. freely routable Stereo Sample Rate Converter), Mdm (2 × 8-Channel Adat Optical-I/O each, plus an 8-Channel Tdif Interface), Stc-1 (Ltc and Vitc sync option with a wide range of possibilities).

- The Core 32 card can be upgraded via the Pc-90 Engine (plug-in), among others. (This plug-in generates multi-effects and reverb at a level of quality comparable to the Pcm-90). A couple of other Lexicon Studio System features worth mentioning are a Time Code input in addition to the internal Word Clock Generator for versatile synchronization with external analog and digital devices.

The new Lexicon system is a hot tip for discerning (and well-heeled, I might add) Vst users. At the time of printing, the Asio driver was projected for release in August '98.

▶ Digidesign's high-end systems ProTools III and ProTools 24 can be classed in the same category as the Lexicon Studio. According to Steinberg, the fortunate owners of this hardware will finally be able to link it directly to Vst/24 by the end of '98 (see ›Which Cubase Version Is Best for You?‹ on page 18). If you're in the enviable position of setting up a first-class Vst system, take the time for a painstaking comparison of the Lexicon Studio and Digidesign's ProTools.

Nubus Alternatives

I've already harped on about the pitfalls of buying an out-dated Nubus Macintosh in the chapter on hardware. If you own one of these computers, you can at least make do with it for a while using Vst. Should your computer be too slow, you can check it out to see if a processor upgrade is feasible or even possible. Upgrade cards with G3 processors are available for Nubus Macintoshes.

There are exactly two possibilities for enhancing the on-board sound system of a Nubus Macintosh. As mentioned earlier, chances are slim that any more are forthcoming—Nubus Macintoshes seem to be an evolutionary dead-end.

Digidesign Audiomedia 2

◆ Nubus, 2 × Analog In and Out each, S/P-Dif I/O, Rca audio ports on the card's slot chassis.

This was the first, and for a long time the only, Nubus audio card for the Macintosh. It is available on the second-hand market only.

An Asio driver is available. In contrast to it's Pci successor, the Audiomedia 3, here you can only use the digital and analog interfaces alternately. The Audiomedia 2 is really just a normal stereo I/O card.

Lucid Technology NB 24

◆ Nubus, S/P-Dif I/O, audio ports on the card's slot chassis, integrated Motorola 56301 Dsp to lighten the Cpu's load.

This is the only Nubus card with a Macintosh Vst Asio driver that is still available in normal retail outlets. It is a slightly stripped-down version of the Lucid Pci card Pci 24 (see page 69). The same description for the Pci 24 holds true for the Nb 24—including the Ada converter recommendation.

The Audiomedia 2 is notorious for its extremely irritable S/P-Dif interfaces. Never, ever swap any cables around while your computer is powered up or the S/P-Dif chip will go up in a puff of smoke! By the way, this is good advice for all other audio cards with integrated S/P-Dif interfaces.

Trendsetters

The audio card market is definitely a tooth-and-nails business. New developments are announced on a daily basis (well, almost) in this most competitive field of virtual studio technology. For a fitting close to this chapter, I would like to introduce you to a couple of promising audio cards for which the VST ASIO driver status is still somewhat ambiguous, but in the long run will most likely be implemented.

Echo Event Darla

Although not immediately apparent, the audio cards by Echo/Event all come complete with an integrated 24-bit Motorola DSP (56301). According to Event, the company is hard at work creating drivers that will unleash the potential of the currently dormant DSPs to provide us impoverished users with additional effects resources.

◆ PCI, 2 × Analog In, 8 × Analog Out, 20-Bit Converter. Audio RCA jacks in an Adapter Box that is mounted directly to the metal slot frame.

Darla is inexpensive and—like all Event cards—according to independent bench tests, has very good audio specifications. If you don't under any circumstances anticipate the need for a digital interface, then Darla comes highly recommenced—once the ASIO driver is available.

Echo Event Gina

◆ PCI, features identical to Darla (2 × Analog In, 8 × Analog Out, 20-Bit Converter), although with additional S/P-DIF I/O, which can be used in parallel in VST (i. e. a max. of 4 × In, 10 × Out). Also features an external box equipped with analog audio interfaces in the form of phone jacks.

This card is not much more expensive than Darla and you get additional digital interfaces for your hard-earned dough. For most users, this will be the preferred version of the two.

Echo Event Layla

◆ PCI, 8 × Analog In, 10 × Analog Out, 20-Bit Converter, S/P-DIF I/O, Wordclock I/O, MIDI-In/Out/Thru, cascadable. Ports housed in an external 19" box.

Currently the most professional of the Event cards and one of the few specimens that features loads of analog audio interfaces.

Mark Of The Unicorn 2408

◆ Pci, external 19" box with 8 × Analog (unbalanced Rca), 2 × Analog Out (balanced, phone), 20-Bit converters; 3 × Adat each and Tdif Interface, 1 × S/P-Dif In, 2 × S/P-Dif Out and Rs-422 interface for synchronization.

◆ A total of seven 8-channel banks (3 × Tascam each and Adat as well as 1 × analog) can be assigned internally to three 8-channel I/O busses, which enables you to access a maximum of 24 simultaneous inputs or outputs, depending on the recording situation.

The MotU system's versatile concept is impressive, as is its price. It retails for somewhere in the range of 1,000 Us dollars, which is unheard of for a system the delivers this level of professional performance. In contrast to the Event cards however, an Asio driver seems a long way off.

▶ It's a good idea to keep an eye on the Asio driver developments for all of these cards. According to Steinberg, in the very near future you can expect a number of interesting audio hardware products featuring Asio drivers to be released. For current info, check out the Wizoo support page for this book (see ›Wizoo Online Support‹ on page 161).

4 So That's What Equalizers Are For

Enough already on boards, drivers and configurations! Now we'll get down to the business at hand and look at the VST mixers in practical applications. Among their most important features are the knobs, faders and other twiddley things that let you voice a signal—i. e. the tone control section often called the filter, equalizer or EQ for short.

Unless you call the depths of a primeval rain forest home, you have presumably encountered a stripped-down version of an EQ in home stereo systems in the form of bass and treble knobs. Your experience with this type of tone control setup might lead you to underestimate the significance of the VST EQs. If you simply use these sound-shaping tools to boost a bit of treble here and there, you are ignoring about 95 % of their capabilities. A fully parametric 4-band EQ like the one in VST is a powerful creative tool. Once you know how to exploit its potential, you'll have made the first step towards the Holy Grail of recording: a professional mixdown.

Regardless of the medium that you are using to shape sound—be it VST, an EQ plug-in or a hardware mixing console—you won't be able to get the job done right until you can at least roughly identify how your EQing efforts affect the frequencies and detect their overall influence on the audio material. For precisely this reason, not only does this book discuss theoretical and practical information, it also features exercises that will help train your hearing so that you will be able to analyze sonic data and pick apart different soundscapes.

The following sections are designed to introduce you to the ›tools of the trade.‹ However, I don't want to get dogmatic about it; once you have a basic handle on the fundamental principles, feel free to break the rules every now and then. There is no hard and fast law that governs how you go about achieving what you have in mind; if you stick to an overly strict set of rules, you'll only stifle your own creative urges.

How Does a Parametric EQ Work?

VST is equipped with so-called ›parametric filter bands,‹ more commonly termed ›parametric EQs.‹ Before we get into the details of what these control features do and how they're handled, we'll take a look at their design. With a parametric filter, you will always shape a ›band,‹ in other words, a specific frequency range. You can manipulate the following parameters:

◆ **Gain:** Also known as ›Presence/Absence‹ or ›Cut/Boost.‹ This parameter determines to which extent you want to attenuate (cut) or amplify (boost) a frequency band; usually the value is expressed in dBs. For the record: At a gain value of 0, the filter doesn't audibly influence the signal.

◆ **Frequency:** This control feature's setting determines the center frequency of the band in Hz or kHz values.

◆ **Q-Factor:** The Q-Factor (Q=quality) determines the width of the affected frequency, imaginatively called the bandwidth. Only when this parameter is infinitely variable is an EQ accurately described as ›fully parametric‹ EQ.

▶ We'll pass on the formula used to calculate the Q-Factor; for one, it's pretty complicated and for the other, it's not interpreted uniformly (›Constant Q,‹ ›Constant Bandwidth‹), which also leads to confusion.

▶ The important thing to keep in mind about the Q-Factor is it's inverse relationship to the filter band: the greater the Q-Factor, the narrower the filter band.

The VST EQ operates in the standard fashion of a parametric EQ—via a bell-shaped filter curve. The effect of a boosted frequency is called a ›peak,‹ a cut frequency is called a ›notch,‹ presumably because this is exactly what they look like in a diagram.

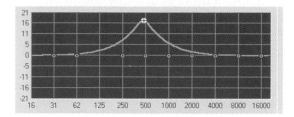

A parametric filter band is determined by gain (degree of boost or cut), frequency (center frequency of the filter curve) and Q (width of the curve).

Which EQ Parameters Do You Need?

VST features four EQ bands—identical in design—for 32 audio channel mixers and 16 group mixer channels. Each activated band costs in terms of computing power. How many of theoretically possible 192 band you can actually use is determined in practice by your computer's performance specs, the amount of effects and the selected EQ quality.

When you're working with filters, you don't have to worry about whether its a stereo or mono channel that you're dealing with: If you are tweaking the EQ of a stereo channel, both sides of the signal are automatically affected. Logically, EQ bands in stereo channels require twice the computing power.

▶ In the VST EQ section, you can also enter gain, frequency and Q values numerically, which is the much more expedient method when you're dealing with precise values: Simply double-click on the number below a given knob and type the desired number on your computer keyboard. Note that fractional—i. e. less than whole-step—increments are preceded by a decimal point (›0.8‹); VST won't let you enter it any other way. In some countries, commas are commonly used to denote decimal values. If you enter a comma for a value, the parameter is reset to the minimum value.

The most important control features in the VST EQ section are the gain, frequency and Q knobs. All others such as ›Limit‹ (the buttons and knobs in the left column of each EQ band) and ›Q-Presets‹ (the four buttons under the Q knob) don't offer any additional functions or parameters. These are

From V. 4.0, VST Macintosh features two hardware-independent audio mixers, or more accurately, mixer sections. In the Audio Channel Mixer, you'll find the ›normal‹ audio mixer channels on the left and the new, baby blue sub-mixer channels on the right. You can also open the latter in the form of an Audio Group Mixer in a separate window (see page 105).

just little helpers; neutralize them by setting ›Hi Limit‹ to the highest value and ›Lo Limit‹ to the lowest value so that you can concentrate on the essential stuff.

These are the essential parameters of the Vst Eq. Everything else is eye-candy.

Which Eq Type for Which Purpose?

From Version 4.0, Vst Macintosh finally lets you select from two completely different Eq types: Next to the old ›thrifty‹ Eq designed specifically to conserve performance power, the program now features another substantially higher-quality algorithm. What exactly are the differences between the two?

Low Quality Eq

The original Vst filter is automatically activated when the High-Quality button is extinguished. This Eq type is on a strict diet when it comes to Cpu power, but it also works in a rather unconventional fashion, to put it mildly. Especially when the gain is cut drastically, the filter curve ›lurches‹ rather drunkenly, as you can clearly see in the illustration on page 86.

When you're working with the filter parameters Gain and Q, you should also be aware that their values are less than reliable. The Gain control range between 0 and approx. ± 4.0

is roughly equivalent to that of a conventional mixing console (ca. ± 15 dB).

Curiously enough, the filter's behave more bizarrely as the values increase. For example, Gain has the greatest influence at values somewhere in the 6.0 range; at higher values, its effect decreases continuously, which is interesting but hardly intentional.

When the internal VsT Q-Factor increments are converted into ›official‹ Q values, it turns out the control range actually lies between 2 (VsT Q value 0.5) and 20 (VsT Q value 0.99). Again, you should only rely on this data to give you rough idea of the values that you're dealing with, because the response of the Q control is affected by Gain and Frequency settings

Even the frequency control—which uses the conventional Hz and kHz values—is a bit wacky: When you cut a frequency, the center frequency of the filter curve is in reality slightly lower than the value selected via the Frequency parameter and vice versa when you dial in a frequency boost. Fascinating but extremely irksome when you're trying to set a frequency precisely to the indicated value.

▶ Take some time to familiarize yourself with the control ranges, but don't rely on the indicated values. Your best bet when you're working with this EQ is to trust your ears; it's just too unpredictable to bet your life's savings on.

▶ When you have the luxury of an option, use this EQ type only to tweak (Gain values up to approx. 2.0) wide frequency ranges (i.e. lowest Q values) subtly. Extreme settings (maximum Q and Gain values) can be useful if you want to create weird sounds in conjunction with effects.

High-Quality-EQ

The new VST EQ is more precise; its phase response is also much truer, so clarity and transparency are enhanced substantially. Definitely use this EQ type when you are mixing acoustic instruments, vocals or mastering a complete mixdown.

You can activate this filter type discretely for every channel via the appropriate button. The EQ setting always applies to all of the channel's active EQ bands. The algorithm is equivalent to that of the 1-band EQ featured in Steinberg's audio editor for Windows PCs, ›WaveLab.‹ Its name is legitimate; compared with the old EQ, it certainly delivers higher-quality performance, but also requires roughly seven times the CPU power.

Although it is a glutton for power, everything else about it is exemplary. In ›official‹ values, the Q parameter of this EQ ranges from 0.5 (VST parameter 0.5) to approx. 50 (VST parameter value 0.99). The control ranges of the Gain and Frequency parameters are equivalent to the official values. The EQ curves respond symmetrically and predictably; overall this EQ simply sounds much better.

With these two EQ algorithms, VST offers a good onboard solution for every recording situation. My recommendation: Use the old EQs primarily during the arrangement phase. You won't have to worry about them hogging too much CPU power in older Macintoshes, and they're definitely good enough to help you come up with a rough idea of the direction the track is going to ultimately take. When you're mixing the track down, you can gradually switch all of the EQs to High-Quality mode.

If you run into CPU-related bottlenecks, use Track Bouncing (see page 145) to load the new EQs settings to individual audio files. Once you have dialed in the optimum filter settings, export them one after the other.

VST-Gain	≈ dB	EQ Response	Application
0.5	approx. 1		Subtle tonal manipulations in wide frequency bands (lowest Q values)
1	approx. 3	Relatively ›benevolent‹ i. e. roughly predictable	
2	approx. 6		›Medium-strength,‹ standard manipulations
3	approx. 12		Audible manipulations
4	approx. 15	›Teetering point‹—At this level, the rest of the spectrum is influenced by approx. 2 to 3 dB.	Prominently audible manipulations, control range threshold of most mixers
5			
6			
7	Maximum at approx. 30 dB to minimum at approx. 14 dB	Conspicuous side effects (negative pulse at the filter frequency)	Drastic manipulations with major side effects, recommended for creating bizarre effects with extremely narrow frequency band settings (high Q value)
8			
9			
10			
11			
12			

▶ The influence of the Gain parameter in the Low-Quality EQ is hard to discern, especially when you're dealing with middle values. For this reason, I recommend that you stick with exceptionally subtle Gain settings, or radical Gain settings when you want to get weird.

A narrow-band cut via the two VST EQs:

The old VST EQ is optimized for operating on minimum CPU power, consequently the filter curve is extremely unbalanced.

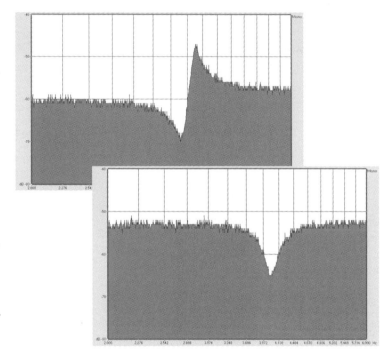

The new High-Quality EQ requires more power, but its quality is better by far and the filter curve is much more symmetrical.

Finding the Right EQ Setting

In the following section, you'll run across phrases such as ›capturing a frequency‹ and ›tuning an EQ.‹ All well and good, but how do you actually handle an EQ? Simply twiddle the knobs? In principle yes, but it is essential that you know where, why and in which order you tweak knobs.

In this aspect, hardware mixers have an advantage over their virtual cousins. In fully parametric EQs, all three parameters are normally assigned to separate knobs. Most people can manipulate two controls at once, more dexterous individuals can even deal with three simultaneously.

In the VST mixer—as in any other audio software—you of course don't have that direct tactile connection, so you have to use a different method. Here's the one that I use to great effect:

1 First you should try to identify the frequency range, so don't be bashful, start with a radical setting. A Gain value of ± 20dB and a Q value of approx. 0.8 in High-Quality mode works fair enough in most cases.

2 Now you can ›tune‹ the EQ, i. e. dial in the desired frequency range via the Frequency parameter. Rotate the knob slowly and listen closely. At which position does the EQ first audibly influence the desired frequency and at which position does the EQ exit this area of influence? The best value for the Frequency parameter is at the center of these two outer limits.

3 Now that you've located the right frequency, you can change the Gain and Q settings at will until you have achieved the desired effect. You can also change the frequency for the sake of comparison. You already know the exact value of the frequency that you were looking for, but sometimes it helps to sweep the knob across frequencies to be able to more accurately judge the influence of different Gain and Q values.

Setting Parameters More Precisely

Changing parameters via knobs and dials on your screen can become a bit tedious after a while. Minor changes in small increments are pretty hard to execute via the mouse. Here's a little trick that should help:

1 Position the EQ that you want to edit at the center of your screen.

2 ›Grab‹ the desired pot, but don't move the cursor directly over it. Instead press and hold the mouse button and drag it to the far border of the screen.

3 Move the cursor along the far border of the screen. Now it should be easy for you to access every parameter increment.

As mentioned earlier, you can type in the values for EQ parameters directly. When you're working with the Alpha Dial of the VST effects tracks, you have no choice but to rely on the mouse, so be sure to use this method.

Search and Destroy: Locating Frequency Ranges

First we'll refresh your possibly long dormant arithmetic skills to gain a better understanding of the numeric relationship of frequencies. The golden rule is easy enough:

◆ A musical interval of one octave is equivalent to double the frequency.

This leads us to two essential conclusions:

Frequency Raster

An ascending octave—start with A at 220 Hz—leads us to the western hemisphere's most popular tone, concert-pitch A at 440 Hz. Way up there in the helium-induced Madonna register, you'll find an A at 7,040 Hz (7.04 kHz). To find the next ascending A, you again have to double the frequency: Yes, there it is at 14,080 Hz (14.08 kHz).

In this example, the octave between the two low A's is only an interval of 220 Hz, the octave between the two high A's a whopping 7,040 Hz.

The lower the frequencies that you want to manipulate, the smaller the frequency increments should be.

What this means when you're EQing is that a slight deviation of the Frequency parameter by just a few Hertz in the bottom has a substantial effect. If you boost a bass frequency somewhere around 60 Hz or 100 Hz, you will notice a huge difference.

On the other hand, when you're working with higher frequencies and you set a Frequency parameter of 14,000 Hz to 14,040 Hz, no one other than possibly your dog will hear the difference. With treble frequencies, you have to think big, for example steps of 100 Hz up to 1 kHz.

Pitch

In tempered tuning, the individual semitone steps have identical intervals between them. Starting with the 440-Hz A, and dividing this number by 12 = approx. 36.7 Hz per semitone step. Here are the frequencies for a major triad with a root at concert-pitch A and an added A an octave higher:

- A = 440 Hz
- #C = approx. 587 Hz = 4 semitones higher
  = 440 Hz + 4 × 36,7 Hz = 586,7 Hz,
- E = approx. 697 Hz = 7 semitones higher
  = 440 Hz + 7 × 36,7 Hz = 696,7 Hz,
- A = 880 Hz = an octave higher = double the original frequency.

This sounds like it has a lot more to do with punching numbers into a calculator rather than music. Not to worry, you don't have to learn all tones and their frequency equivalents to thirteen places after the decimal point by rote. Just keep the basic principle in mind, it will help you to ›design‹ sounds and eliminate unwanted frequencies.

▶ Finally, it's time for your ears to get a workout. We'll now work with the songs and audio examples on the included CD-ROM. If you skipped the mini-manual covering the CD, you should go back and check it out—you'll find it on page 11.

1 Loop the sine chord and open the EQ.

2 Try to find the optimum EQ settings so you can influence each tone in the chord individually, i.e. without affecting the others. You can use the formula discussed above to calculate the frequencies: The lowest tone has a frequency of 220 Hz, the highest, 440 Hz.

◎ **02**—A descending major triad with an added octave and a concert-pitch root played in sine tones.

As you have just experienced, you have to work with relatively narrow frequency bands—i. e. a high Q-Factor—so you don't address all of the tones at once. However, EQing is not nearly as convenient as this example might lead you to believe. In real-world applications, you will find it exceeding difficult to isolate individual tones via EQ.

◎ **03**—It actually works: One of the four EQ bands for every note in the chord. You can manipulate the volume of the individual tones via the Gain controls.

At low frequencies, minor frequency deviations are more prominent than at high frequencies. This is illustrated more clearly in the logarithmic scale (top) than in the linear scale (bottom). Both illustrations depict a frequency analysis of the sine chord featured in Example 02.

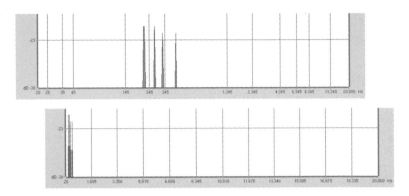

Selecting the Right Q Factor

A sine tone is like Cousin Fred, the accountant. It's boring beyond belief because it consists solely of the root tone, and like Fred who has no other interests, the sine tone doesn't have any other sonic components. This is why a sine tone is represented on the frequency scale by nothing more than a vertical line. All other types of tones feature additional overtone content. The root tone determines the pitch and the overtone structure determines the timbre or tonal color. The brighter or livelier a tone, the greater its overtone content. Obviously, if a tone is chock-full of overtones, it's frequencies will be all over the place on the frequency spectrum. This has the following ramifications when you're selecting a suitable Q-Factor:

High Q values (10—100): Extremely narrow filter bands seriously upset the natural balance between the root tone and overtones. In most cases, this type of EQ will make acoustic instruments and vocals sound artificial. Extremely high Q values are used for a drastic ›fix‹ in the mix—for example to kill feedback in a live recording or to create wacky effects.

Middle Q values (4—10): This value range comes in pretty handy when you want to influence individual aspects of a sound, for instance to accentuate the low-end rumble, fat mids or silky highs when you're mixing a cello sound.

Low Q values (0.5—4): You should use relatively wide filter bands for global EQing tasks such as ›beef it up a bit‹ or ›needs a little more high end sparkle.‹ You'll notice that your manipulations are less intrusive and more subtle because the original timbre remains pretty much intact. The result is usually more pleasing, more musical.

To get a feel for how different Q values sound in combination with various Gain and Frequency settings, you should mess around with the next examples for a while.

1 On Track 1/2 of Example 05, you'll find two-bar sequences of the original mixdown. Loop the first sequence and focus on the timbre or tonal color of the sequence.

2 Mute Track 1/2 and listen to the first EQed sequence on Track 3/4. Switch Track 1/2 back on and try to ›bend‹ the loop via an EQ band so that it sounds like the sequence on Track 3/4.

3 To monitor your progress, switch back and forth between Tracks 3/4 and 1/2, until you're confident that you have come up with something close to the EQed sequence. You'll find the exact settings that we used expressed as EQ parameter values on page 171.

4 Follow the same procedure for all other tracks. Note the influence of different Q and frequency values.

As you can see, even with just a single filter band, EQing is not an easy task. With practice, you'll be able to create similar exercises to the one we just ran through, although using two or more filter bands simultaneously.

Using EQs Creatively

An EQ is a pretty handy little tool, you can use it for much more than just to iron out the bugs in an audio recording. It is also a creative instrument that is well-suited for generating

Don't confuse the scale of the VST Q parameter with the ›official‹ Q values described above. Even the High-Quality EQ operates on a rather steep scale. For normal tonal corrections, you'll find that relatively low Q parameter values between 0.5 and 0.6 will in most cases deliver the best results.

◎ **04**—The original version of a mixdown loop.

◎ **05**—Different EQ settings -imitations invited.

An EQ doesn't magically conjure up frequencies, it simply changes existing frequencies. In other words, you can only EQ a frequency range if it is actually there in the audio material that you're dealing with. This rule is as elementary as it is universally applicable to all types EQing!

sound effects. The following section discusses a few of the more unusual EQ applications.

Sound Design via EQ

06—A hi-hat track is a ›noisy‹ sound that lends itself to radical EQ settings to achieve weird effects.

1 First listen to the original version of the hi-hat loop and then open the EQ.

2 Activate the four bands, one after the other. Tune the frequencies in octaves (double each of them), which gives you an interesting mix of tonal and noise characteristics.

07—These type of extreme manipulations work well in mixes that otherwise sound rather staid.

Experiment with other noisy sounds. With narrow-band filters, you can emphasize individual frequencies so that they really pop out of the mix.

Balancing Levels via EQ

1 First listen to the drum loop and then open the EQ.

08—A drum loop that would be great for a song, if only the kick drum sounded better.

2 Try to dial in an EQ setting that captures the kick drum so that you can attenuate it without affecting other frequencies in the loop. Vary the EQ parameters and note the different effects.

3 Add another kick drum to the mix in the desired groove, e.g. by playing it on a MIDI sound generating device.

09—Here you can use the Gain control of the first filter band to fade the bass drum out.

This type of manipulation will rarely sound perfect, but when heard in the context of other signals (e. g. when you overdub a new kick drum or bass later on), it usually does the trick.

Separating Tracks via EQ

This example takes the previous example a step further. It is definitely more advanced and demonstrates a technique that will let you dial in some pretty wild effects:

10—Another drum loop destined for the meat grinder.

1 Assign the audio region to parallel positions in two different mono tracks.

11—Here's something you could come up with: EQ separation with a sneak preview of the chapter on effects.

2 Set the EQS so that only the kick drum is audible in one track and solely the hi-hat in the other.

3 Slap different effects on the two tracks.

Generating Pseudo Stereo via EQ

1 Assign the audio region to parallel positions in two different mono tracks.

2 For both tracks, activate all four frequency with a medium Q value. Spread the Frequency parameters of the four bands relatively wide (e.g. 400 Hz, 1 kHz, 2.5 kHz and 6 kHz).

3 Boost the first and third band and cut the second and fourth band in one channel. Set up the opposite EQ Gain configuration in the other channel.

4 Set the one channel's Panorama to the far left, the other to the far right.

The majority of these examples are of course not what you might call subtle; quite the opposite actually. But keep in mind that radical EQing is usually more effective when you limit it to individual components in the mix. For example, if you seriously bend a hi-hat, it is usually a good idea to add another unprocessed hi-hat that plays a different groove to the other side of the mix, otherwise the effect will sound artificial or somewhat strained.

◎ **12**—Mono strings that might sound better in stereo.

◎ **13**—Much improved sound: Pseudo stereo via EQ. The difference is especially evident when you monitor via headphones and press the Mono button in the Master section.

An Overview of the Frequency Ranges

Human hearing is very sensitive, but certainly doesn't work like a precision measuring instrument. You will detect some frequency ranges readily, whereas others have to be very much ›in your face‹ before you take note of them.

We'll let acoustic engineers worry about loudness, evaluation curves, phon and sone; instead we'll get down to the business of finding out what subjective hearing means in terms of EQing. To close out this chapter, we'll take a quick tour through the more prominent ranges of the frequency spectrum:

20 Hz to 60 Hz

Subbass with ultra-low frequencies is hip; techno-heads, trip-hoppers and ravers especially enjoy frequencies low and loud enough to cause massive cardiac arrest. All well and good, but keep in mind that when you want to work with these frequencies, you have to have equipment that is capable of reproducing heavy-duty bottom end rumble. You'll need special subwoofers that are normally found in large PA systems only. So unless you coincidentally happen to have a huge PA lying around the house, go easy on these frequencies unless you are working with special dance mixdowns.

Besides, the majority of instruments simply won't give you the kind of oomph you are presumably after, so if you're into ultra-low basses, you will have to invest in special Fx devices or plug-ins (subbass generators).

60 Hz to 100 Hz

Even in many high-end hardware mixing consoles, 60 Hz is the EQ's bottom limit. And with good reason, this is low enough for virtually every musical style other than the newer electronica-type stuff. As discussed earlier, the range between 60 and 100 Hz is very sensitive. This is where you normally tune the bass. Keep in mind that the differences are very audible say between an EQ boost at 60 Hz or at 80 Hz. Carefully tune the filter when you're EQing the bottom end and choose the sweet spot, i. e. where the bass signal delivers the biggest punch and the least mud.

As usual, there is a drawback: You won't hear much of a difference until you invest in a good, expensive set of monitors.

When you're working with small nearfield monitors, the only thing that will help you out is experience. Try out different settings while you're mixing and jot down notes on each EQ configuration. Listen to your mixes through larger speakers, a car stereo and if at all possible a large PA system. This is the only way that you will get a feel for what the bass EQ should sound like on your tiny monitor speakers so that the mix delivers the goods over large systems. Sound far-fetched? I've relied on this method for years now. You can actually mix tracks down using small Yamaha Ns-10 speakers and get results that sound great over other systems. Believe me, it works.

100 Hz to 200 Hz

This is the singles bar for frequencies, the range where bass and low mids meet and mingle. It's a cool place to tweak bass signals in this range. For example, if you have recorded a really low, grumbling and rumbling bass line, you should position the kick drum a bit higher in the frequency spectrum; somewhere around 160 Hz is a good place to start.

200 Hz to 1 kHz

You will find that the midrange is the frequency zone that is definitely the biggest challenge during mixdown. It really is difficult to get handle on, so your best bet is hands off unless you're having a major problem with the composite mix, i. e. the different tracks sound shoddy when you play them back together.

Here's one extreme: Your mix sounds muddy and cluttered. This often happens when you have to record under difficult conditions (live) or use low-quality gear. The reason for this phenomenon is that your recording will be chock full of mids; even the cheapest dictaphone will record these. The other frequencies such as truly low basses and high-resolution highs are missing altogether simply because they weren't recorded in the first place. Listen to the different tracks, identify those with an inordinate amount of mids and try to cut these frequencies.

The other extreme: You've ended up with loads of bottom end punch, but the entire recording sounds cold or artificial. Often, all that you need is a healthy helping of low mids to make the mix sound warmer or more natural. In contrast to the problem discussed above where too many mids have an identifiable cause; an absence of mids—like disappearing drummers—is not due to spontaneous combustion. Check if you didn't actually cause the problem yourself by going over-board while EQing the tracks.

The quality that these frequencies are responsible for is best described as warmth. This range is crucial to vocals and electric guitars. If the former lacks mids, the voices will sound like that one ex: cold and synthetic. If the latter doesn't have enough mids in the mix, you'll end up with an accurate imitation of an electric razor, especially when you used a DI box rather than mic an amp. If you run into this type of problem, subtly boost the frequencies somewhere in the range of 300 Hz to melt some of the ice.

1 kHz to 3 kHz

If the frequency range is a neighborhood, you have just entered the house of pain. Our hearing is especially sensitive to this frequency range and, like no other, it has the capacity to seriously slice into your central nervous system. If you find that a signal is too cutting or edgy, cut the frequencies in the 1—2 kHz range. In almost every case, this will fix the mix.

On the other hand, if you take no prisoners and eradicate all of the lower highs, you will end up with the aural equiva-lent of a soft, fuzzy sweater. If the mix sounds like too much fabric softener and not enough starch, dial in a dose of this frequency range.

3 kHz to 12 kHz

This is the frequency range normally associated with the higher end. In terms of treble, the majority of energy is transported in this slice of the frequency pie. Here you shouldn't be attempting to capture entire instruments, instead concentrate on those parts of the signal that lend the sound some sparkle. If a guitar sounds dead, the string section as if they forgot to wax their strings or your vocalist like a cobra, fix these problems via these frequencies.

12 kHz to 20 kHz

We're way up there now. The higher you go, the brighter, shinier the highs. At the same time, you're pushing the limits of human hearing and what speaker systems can reproduce. A compromise is your best bet here.

If your mixdown lacks sheen or sparkle, boost these frequencies. 12 kHz is a good place to start, move up in frequencies as the situation dictates. Again, you can only boost what is actually there. Ride cymbals, vocals and of course similar synth sounds are well-served by a healthy helping of upper end frequencies.

▶ I can't give you an example of the ideal CD, and I don't have to: The best example is your favorite song. Import it from CD and see what happens when you boost or cut the different frequency ranges discussed above. This is a great exercise that you should repeat constantly with all kinds of different audio material to train your ear for your own mixdowns! Unless of course you have minor irritations that limit your free time such as a job, family and friends—in this case, repeat the exercise as often as possible.

5 Software Effects Racks

From way back in early days, among the coolest features of VST were the internal software effects. These run in realtime without requiring additional budget-busting DSP hardware.

With Version 4.0, Macintosh users finally have access to both standard studio methods of effects routing: Patching signals to effects via sends (aux circuits) and looping in effects to signals via inserts.

Routing Signals to Effects via Sends

In all channels the Channel Mixer features eight send circuits, which engineers also like to call aux circuits. These circuits let you route a signal to a maximum of eight different effects. These signal paths are handled in the same manner that you would deal with aux circuits in a hardware mixer.

You can access the requisite functions via a double-click on the Fx button of a channel. Activate pop-ups that are located under each channel send knob to select one of the eight effects devices that you want to route the signal to and the circuit that you want to use for this purpose. This is a very special feature that gives the experienced VST user more signal routing options. However, it is also a source of much confusion to newbies:

♦ You will always choose from a maximum of eight effects that are active in the effects rack. VST is unkind, it doesn't care whether the effects devices are switched on or off. If you select an effects device that is switched off, the send signal ends up in software limbo.

♦ VST won't argue with you if you assign several send knobs to the same effects device. It will however note which

To make it a bit easier for you to get a handle on this topic, we'll look at the basic VST functions, i.e. the functions that apply to the Channel Mixer. We'll look at some more special applications in conjunction with the Group Mixer and how you can expand your options in the section ›Special Fx with the Group Mixer‹ on page 103.

send circuit was activated first and route the signal exclusively via this circuit. The second send signal is ignored until you either switch the first signal off or turn it all the way down. If you're not careful when you configure your signal routing setup, Vst's priority programming may lead to a situation where you have an active effects send circuit that has no influence on an active effects device.

▶ In addition to addressing a Send effects or master stereo signal, each send knob for special applications can also route signals to the Group channels (see ›Routing Sends to Group Channels‹ on page 109).

If you're new to the Vst mixer, you should leave the pop-up presets as they are for the time being. The visuals will be less confusing simply because the control elements remain in a logical array: The left send knobs control—from top to bottom—the upper four effects devices in the send rack, and the right send knobs control the lower four effects devices (numbers five through eight).

Pre- and Post-Fader Mode

Each of the eight Send circuits in every channel is equipped with a Pre button. Use it to determine the mode in which the corresponding Send knob operates:

◆ Post-Fader: If the Pre button is extinguished, the Send signal is routed out after (Post) the channel fader. The latter influences the Send signal as well as the Send knob. When you pull the channel fader all the way down, the Send level is zero.

◆ Pre-Fader: If the Pre button is illuminated, the Send signal is routed out before (Pre) the channel fader. In this case, the Send amount depends solely on the position of the Send knob.

Keep in mind that in Post-Fader mode—much like a shotgun wedding—the direct signal (the dry signal that is controlled by the channel fader) and the effects signal (called wet in audio jargon) are automatically inseparable. This is usually the desired configuration, so you might say that Post-Fader is the standard operating mode.

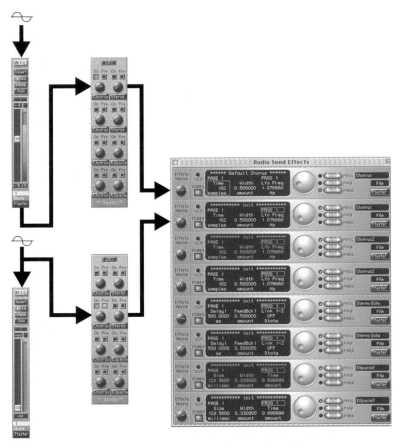

In Post-Fader mode (top), the effects send signal is routed out after the channel fader; in Pre-Fader mode, prior to the fader. In the latter case, you can work with the signal even when the channel fader is pulled all the way down.

In Post-Fader mode, the extreme fader position—i. e. pulled all the way down—is essential. In this case, none of the dry signal is audible, you will hear exclusively the wet effects signal. You can manipulate the wet signal level independently of the dry signal via the Send knob.

Patching in Effects via Inserts

You have an alternative to routing signals to effects via send circuits; you can patch in effects via inserts. Much like in an effects loop, the signal chain is ›severed,‹ the dry signal is re-routed through one or more effects devices and the wet signal is ›spliced‹ back into the signal circuit. Current versions of Vst feature two types of Insert effects racks:

◆ Master Effects: There is only one master rack and logically enough, it is accessible via the master circuit only. In contrast to the Send rack, in which eight effects devices operate completely independently, here the signal runs through four effects in series, starting at the top and working its way down. If more than one effects device is active, then the output signal of the top device is routed to the input of the next device below it and so forth.

◆ Channel/Group Inserts: This rack is available in every mono channel or stereo channel pair of the Channel Mixer and in every stereo channel of the Group Mixer. In other words, with 32 mono channels and eight stereo groups, you have forty racks at your disposal. The input signal is routed out after the channel Eq so that the channel tone controls influence the effects signal. The signal is then routed through a maximum of four effects in series. The output signal of the final Insert effect is routed back to the channel prior to the Pan control.

The Right Effects Routing

Other than maybe contemplating why all of this stuff is so complicated, the crucial question that you will have when you're working with the VST effects rack is, ›What type of effects routing scheme is best for which purpose and why?‹

Send Post-Fader

With the Send circuit, you can route as many channel signals through a single effects device as you like. This is a pretty nifty attribute when you are using seriously CPU-hungry plug-ins.

Post-Fader mode is a sensible solution for all effects that you slap on direct signals as a bit of icing on the cake; reverb and delay immediately come to mind as suitable treatments.

Send Pre-Fader

This special mode is primarily suited to two applications:

♦ Say you want to send several signals through a single effect of the Send effects rack and you want to hear just the wet signal, e. g. different guitar tracks through the same chorus. Set all channel faders for all guitar tracks to zero, set the Send knobs for the chorus plug-in to Pre and balance out the levels of the guitar signals via the diverse Send knobs.

♦ Say you want to record effects signals separately from the original signals. In this case, Pre-Fader Send mode is a good option if the plug-ins are not equipped with knobs that control the effects balance and/or you want to use several effects simultaneously and in parallel. (see ›The Miracle Worker: Track Bouncing‹ from page 145 on-wards).

Channel Insert

This is the type of circuit you should use when you *do not* want to mix the wet effects signal to the dry signal, but would rather insert (hence the name) the effects signal into the signal circuit.

The preferred type of effects for inserts are so-called signal processors—compressors, gates or limiters. EQ plug-ins and exciters will work too.

Master Effects

In my experience, I've found that every conceivable type of signal processing or effect delivers much better results when you apply it to a specific signal or group of signals. The section ›Special Fx with the Group Mixer‹ on page 105 explains how this works.

In principle, the same observations on the channel Inserts apply here, except that this is an insert to the master bus. Be wary of any miracle-working stereo master signal manipulation, it generally won't (work). Any type of editing of the finished mixdown should be done as a separate task.

Your best bet for plug-ins to the master bus are primarily displays such as virtual tuning devices or analytic tools that let you check out essential signal characteristics such as frequency response or degree of correlation.

Serial and Parallel Effect Combinations

Another thing that you should keep in mind is that effects in the Send effects rack operate up in parallel and effects in the Master effects or an Insert rack operate in series. This lets you combine different effects so that you can build your own complex multi-effect. Here are some practical examples for both of the circuit types.

Serial Effects Combination with Insert

◎ **14**—Too much of a good thing—a squeaky clean E-piano synth sound.

◎ **15**—A combination of two Choirus 2's can do the trick: An actual living, breathing Wurlitzer.

1   Open the Insert rack for the channel that you want to work with. For the time being, activate the top effects device only. For example, select Choirus 2 and dial in the desired settings.

2   Activate additional effects in the Insert rack, e.g. the Electro Fuzz (Yeah!) or another Choirus 2 to beef up the sound. Work in methodical steps so things don't get out of hand.

Parallel Effects Combination with Send

1   Open the Send effects rack and position different effects there, e.g. Stereo Echos and Auto Pan.

2 Route the signal to the effects in Post-Fader mode. Dial in the desired settings at the effects device, turn its input (or the corresponding send circuit) down and set up the next effect.

3 Don't turn the effects input back up until you've finished. In the meantime, experiment with different send settings.

Using several effects for a single signal is not a luxury reserved for wealthier high-end Macintosh owners. You can have your box compute and then store the effects signals to free up Cpu resources. What's more, you can use this procedure to design much more complex effects combinations (see ›The Miracle Worker: Track Bouncing‹ from page 145 onwards).

◎ **16**—A nice little synth arpeggio, but dry as a Sahara water hole.

◎ **17**—Cool arpeggios via two Stereo Echos and Auto Pan.

Special Fx with the Group Mixer

The Group Mixer, a new feature of Vst 4.0 Macintosh, plays a key role in effects routing. It expands Vst by eight additional stereo channels, which give you much more versatile signal routing options.

Activating the Group

In contrast to the ›normal‹ channels in the Channel Mixer, Group channels are color-coded in blue. These are located to the right of the Channel Mixer. If desired, you can also open these in a separate window via Audio Group Mixer in the Panels menu.

In the Vst default setup, the Group channels are ignored, as illustrated by the fact that for every ›normal‹ channel of the Channel Mixer, ›Master‹ is indicated at the bottom of its display. This means that the output signal of the channel is routed directly to the Vst stereo master signal and the Group channels are simply disregarded.

To change this status, click on the one of the channel's Master fields mentioned above. A pop-up menu will do just that—pop up. In it, you can select any of the eight stereo

Group channels instead of Master. If for example you select Grp 1, the channel output signal is not routed directly to the Master stereo signal, but to the first stereo Group channel.

If Master is indicated at the bottom of this channel's display, then the channel's output signal is routed to the Vst Master signal. The Group channel is thus an insert between the outputs of the ›normal‹ channels and the Vst stereo master signal. This is a neat little feature that you can use for kinds of nifty routing tricks.

Level Control via Subgroups

The first function that comes to mind for the Group channels is to use them as so-called ›subgroups‹ found in many hardware mixing consoles. These are used to assign similar signals to a group—for instance, all instruments in a drum set, the Channel Mixer to Group Stereo Channel 1, all harmony vocals to Group 2, all rhythm guitars to Group 3 etc.

You can continue to control the balance between the individual drum instruments in the usual manner in the Channel Mixer, but when you want to turn the volume for the entire drum set up or down, all you have to do is tweak the Group 1 fader.

Obviously, you don't have to send all signals via the Group channels. Use these only for practical signal groups and route the rest of the normal channels directly to the Stereo Master in the usual manner.

Other Channel Functions

The Group channels come complete with more than just faders, you get the whole shebang. Just as we described above the volume level, you can use any channel function simultaneously for all signals that are routed to a Group channel:

◆ Mute/Solo: Often you'll find that the Group channels are worth having just for these control options. Not only is silencing all drums via a single click of a button more elegant, it's also a heck of lot faster than working your way through eight or more channels.

▶ Keep this method in mind when you want to record mute events via the mixer automation. Not only can you set a Group mute more precisely, you'll also find it much easier to post-edit a single event rather than a bunch of individual mutes (see ›Mixer Automation‹ on page 138).

◆ EQ: See if you can filter entire signal groups—e. g. all backing vocal channels—rather than individual signals. The former is more comfortable and conserves CPU power.

◆ Insert: An Insert effect in a Group channel is often the better solution for effects routing in Pre-Fader Send mode (see page 103) simply because it's a less complex procedure to patch several signals as a group through a chorus or flanger.

For most signal processor plug-ins (e. g. compression or stereo manipulations), the Master effects rack is not the ideal solution. In virtually all cases, you'll be better off slapping the effect on a select group of signals. That's exactly what the Group channel option will let you when you use the effect in its Insert rack.

Cascading Group Channels

Up to this point, we've assumed that the output of Group channel is routed directly to the Master section. This is not the law—you can also route every Group output to another Group input.

This option lets you cascade channels, e. g.: Channel 1—6 ⇨ Group 1 ⇨ Group 2 ⇨ Master.

Here a signal is piped through a series of several channels, so your sound-shaping options increase considerably. With two Group channels, you have a total of 8 (4 + 4) EQ bands and 8 (4 + 4) insert circuits at your disposal.

Even if you cascade just two channels, your routing options are so much more flexible: For example, the Insert rack in channel is always routed pre-Send knob. Say you wanted to send a signal through a distortion unit via an insert and then add a bit of reverb via a send. You won't have go through all kinds of signal routing acrobatics because the Send knob is located after the Insert—all you have to do is dial in some reverb over the distorted signal.

◆ **Insert/Send:** For a variation on the above configuration with two cascaded Group channels, try this on for size: Route the first Group channel's Send circuit to the reverb. Be sure to use a circuit where the original signal is clean, i. e. without distortion. Place the Electro Fuzz in the Insert rack of Group 2. It adds dirt to the original dry signal only, while the reverb makes the clean signal roomier.

◆ **Send/EQ:** You also have more liberal EQing options: Normally, these are located pre-Send knobs and thus influence the Send portion of the signal. If you cascade two Group channels, you can control the level of the desired Sends via the first channel and filter the original signal with EQs in the second channel. In other words, you are EQing the dry signal, but not the wet Send signal.

The normal VST signal bus system is designed to get the job for the vast majority of applications. The options we looked at above are more esoteric signal swapping tricks that you should only use when you know exactly what you are trying to achieve. Go ahead and experiment with the different possibilities to hear what they will let you come up.

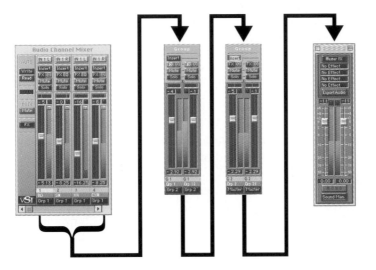

Serial cascading of Group Mixer channels lets you come up with extremely bizarre signal routing setups. But before you go hog wild and route signals all over the place, work with the standard stuff for a while until you get the hang of it. There will be plenty of time for this type of trickery when you are a more advanced VST user.

Routing Sends to Group Channels

The routing buttons mentioned earlier—the ones that let you send a signal to a Group channel—are not just found in the channels of the Channel Mixer. You can also access the Groups via the Send knob pop-up-menus (see ›Routing Signals to Effects via Sends‹ on page 99).

If you select a Group from this type of menu, then the Send knob controls the amount of the signal that is sent to the selected Group channel. This signal routing combination of Groups and Send knobs is primarily suitable for two operations:

♦ Here you can ›duplicate‹ a signal and send the clones to different Group channels without actually copying the audio files. This might come in handy if you're a glutton for effects and the eight normal effects sends aren't enough for your appetite. You can get into all kinds of complicated routing fun-n-games such as filtering the channels differently and sending the filter signals to different effects, using different insert effects in parallel and so forth.

▶ Keep in mind that when you overlap signals by sending the same signal via parallel circuits to an output, weird phase cancellations may occur. Always check if the master signal sounds washed our or unduly colored.

◆ The Effects send rack in VST works with a mono input. If you at some point invest in a high-quality reverb plug-in with a stereo input and output, you can use the Groups as true stereo effects racks: Say you have a stereo signal on Channels 1/2 of the Channel Mixer which you want to slap a dab of reverb on. Select Send Knob 1 in Channel 1 for the destination Group 1. In Channel 2, define Group 2 for Send Knob 5 located to the right (I select it only because it's more practical). Now if you place a ›true‹ stereo plug-in in the Insert rack of Group Channels 1/2, you end up with a fully-fledged stereo effects send setup.

The same method serves to use the entire Group Mixer as a ›true stereo multi-effects device‹ with the wildest routing and stacking options.

▶ I can't emphasize enough that the Group Mixer is recommended to advanced users only. This is why you won't find any special CD examples—I didn't want to send you into the ›fray‹ before you're ready. If you are nonetheless determined to experiment with it, CD examples 10 to 17 and 39/40 are pretty good templates. You can copy all of these routings using the Group Mixer's special capabilities. Go ahead and give it a shot—but later, much later!

Avoiding Errors in the Group Mixer

Most functions that give you more versatile options are also inevitably a source of confusion. The Group Mixer is no exception. You should keep the following in mind, particularly if you've never worked with hardware mixing consoles featuring similar functions:

◆ **Level:** As soon as you route a channel from the Channel Mixer to a Group channel, obviously this signal is no longer routed directly to the stereo Master signal. If the selected Group channel is muted or the fader drawn all the way down, you will come across a situation you might not be accustomed to: The channel meter in the Channel Mixer will cheerfully bounce back and forth, but you won't hear a sound. In this case, don't panic, simply check out the Group Mixer to see what's up!

◆ **Panorama:** You could say much the same for Panorama. If you route stereo signals to the Group channels, make sure the Pan controls are wide open (left channel to the left, right channel to the right). Otherwise you'll lose the original stereo position of the channel signals and everything will be piped right through the middle.

◆ **Insert:** The problem with using Mono-In plug-ins in stereo channels pertains to all stereo Groups. If at all possible, use ›true‹ stereo in/out plug-ins only and try to gain a very clear picture of the signal routing setup in your mind (see ›Channel/Group Insert Racks‹ on page 115).

◆ **Cᴘᴜ load:** In the Group Mixer, it's tremendously tempting to pile on the additional Eǫ bands and effects plug-ins. And why not, after all, that's what it's there for. On the other hand, going overboard on the sonic toys will quickly do an overkill number on your computer's Cᴘᴜ. Assess your setup carefully—rather than using several similar Group Mixer insert plug-ins, will a single send effect get the job done?

Again, these and other considerations lead me to recommend that Vsᴛ newbies forget about the Group Mixer for the time being. If you are just getting into the game, play with the signal flow in the ›normal‹ audio Channel Mixer until you've got it down pat and then move on to the Group Mixer.

Plug-in Signal Flow

You'll be able to do quite a lot with just the information on plug-ins provided earlier. However, we'll take a closer look at the signal flow through the plug-ins so you don't run into any perplexing problems when you are trying more advanced or wilder experiments.

In practice, there are three basic variations on the structure of effects plug-ins:

Stereo In/Out

This is the deluxe edition. An effect that accepts a stereo signal at its input, processes it internally without mashing the two sides together into mono mush and routes the signal back out in stereo is rather unimaginatively called a ›true stereo effect.‹

You should use this type of plug-in when you want to process audio material where the stereo information is already clearly audible in the original signal and you consider it a crucial factor, for example during final mixdown. Only then will the spatial characteristics of the stereo soundscape remain completely intact.

Vst Macintosh features just three specimens of this species of plug-in. Scopion is a display instrument; Wizard and Externalizer manipulate stereo characteristics. If you have a craving for a true stereo reverb plug-in or a stereo compressor, you'll have to look to third-party vendors.

Mono In/Out

In peripheral racks, effects devices with mono inputs and outputs are not exactly state of the art. This holds true for effects where spatial data is crucial only. Effects such as Eq or compressors are ideal in Mono in/out versions, provided of course that you use them exclusively to process mono signals. Other effect types such as chorus or delay in mono are just fine for many applications.

Bona fide mono effects are exactly what you want to use if you are processing a mono signal and do not want to manipulate its spatial characteristics. The Vst Electro Fuzz is an example of this type of plug-in.

Mono In/Stereo Out

This ›hybrid‹ specimen is often sighted in typical plug-in habitats. The effect in this type of device generates or adds a stereo signal when you patch in a mono signal.

This version is great if you want to take a mono signal and manipulate its 3D image, i. e. make it wider or deeper. The majority of reverb algorithms work according to this principle and the Vst-internal Espacial and WunderVerb 3 are no exceptions.

Remarkably, it's not all that easy to tell offhand to which of these three groups a plug-in belongs to. For the time being, trust me on this. The plug-ins that I used as examples are indeed typecast correctly. Once you've read the next chapter, you'll be able to figure out the structure of a plug-in on your own.

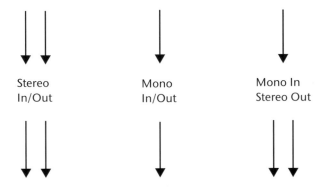

Stereo
In/Out

Mono
In/Out

Mono In
Stereo Out

The three primary plug-in types. The middle type is available with one or two ›virtual outputs.‹ However, the two signals routed to the two outputs are identical.

Routing Traps

Now you know the theory—which type of plug-in structure is best for the different applications—but in practice, you'll run into some more questions that you'll need answers to:

◆ Is there a menu for each plug-in where you can select the type of structure that you would prefer?

◆ Can you ›install‹ any plug-in to every Vsт effects rack?

◆ Is every plug-in structure supported optimally for every type of routing option?

The answers are easy, it sounds exactly like what your mom used to say all the time: ›No, no and again no.‹ The ramifications are however more complex. For one, the structure of a plug-in is limited to one or two options and you often don't know what these might be. For the other, depending on the type of routing option that you use, you will encounter certain conflicts or limitations. The golden rule is:

◆ The weakest link in the signal chain is decisive.

If you place a plug-in with a stereo input in an effects rack that will only admit mono signals, then of course you won't be able exploit the advantages of the plug-in. On the other hand, a stereo circuit won't do you much good if your plug-in can only process mono signals.

Sounds logical enough, doesn't it? Well, it's not that easy. Put on your Sherlock Holmes outfit and join me as we examine the mysteries of effects signal routing via plug-ins:

Send Effects Rack

Here you can use any type of plug-in that you see fit. However, you have to watch for a devious routing trap: The Send effects rack does feature a stereo out, but the send circuits that route signals to the effects inputs are mono. Here Vsт will only allow you to use plug-ins with mono inputs.

Don't curse the mixer, mono send circuits are standard equipment. Even in real-world hardware mixers, true stereo sends are few and far between. You'll have to shell out an exorbitant amount of money for a high-end console to enjoy this luxury.

▶ If you send a stereo signal in Pre-Fader mode to the send rack while the channel fader is in the down position, all of the spatial characteristics of the direct (dry) signal will be lost! This scenario is however very unusual; you probably won't encounter it too often in practice.

Nevertheless, there is a method that will allow you to address true stereo plug-ins in VST via stereo send circuits; it is explained in the section ›Routing Sends to Group Channels‹ on page 109.

Master Effects Rack

The signal that is routed through this effects rack is the stereo master signal, so unless you're going for a pre-sixties type of sound, you definitely don't want any plug-ins to reduce the signal to mono. The only type of plug-in that will do is one that is equipped with stereo ins and outs.

Whereas in other situations, VST gives you the cold shoulder, here it is a watchdog: It will only let you select this type of plug-in for this rack such as the Scopion or Wizard.

Channel/Group Insert Racks

Just as with the Send rack, here you have a free choice of plug-ins. But make no mistake, your freedom of choice isn't nearly as free as we'd all like it to be. You have to be aware of exactly what you're dealing with. When you're using Insert racks in the Channel Mixer, you have to know whether you are routing an Insert effect to a mono or stereo channel:

◆ **Mono channel:** You shouldn't run into any problems if you're using Mono in/out plug-ins simply because you're dealing with apples only: the signal, channel and plug-in formats are identical. If you want or have to throw in an orange—a plug-in equipped with a stereo out—be aware that you can only use the left side of the effect. This setup can lead to all kinds of confusion if your stereo plug-in features separate meters and parameter displays for the two stereo channels. Among other frustrating side-effects, you can dial away at the plug-in parameters for the right channel until the cows come home; nothing will happen. Haughty Vsт simply ignores the right plug-in channel completely.

◆ **Stereo channel:** In stereo channels, you'll find that the Stereo Insert rack is designed for both channels, which is why only one Insert button exists for both channels. For this application, a stereo in/out plug-in is undoubtedly your best bet. If you decide to use a plug-in equipped with a mono input, then only the left channel of the direct signal is processed by the effect, and the right channel is automatically muted.

▶ The Group Mixer features stereo channels exclusively. The second point discussed above applies to it as well.

As you can well imagine, all of this can lead to chaos when you use insert effects in stereo channels. It's a good idea to try out the response of different plug-in types used in conjunction with a stereo channel insert and see for yourself.

Checking Out a Plug-in's Signal Flow

With the help of the following ›testing tools,‹ you can check out any plug-in to see which type that you're dealing with:

Stereo In/Out

18—A stereo test file where logic reigns supreme: ›Left‹ is spoken on the left and ›Right‹ on the right channel.

1   Listen to the stereo file without any effects to hear if the two spoken words sound on the proper sides. If they don't, then you've crossed wires somewhere in your monitor circuit. Locate the problem and rectify it.

2   Place the Wizard in the Insert rack of stereo channel 1-2 and activate it. You will continue to hear both stereo sides, only with some added filtering or distortion. The Wizard does not encroach upon the stereo signal of the original audio material.

3 Now activate the Wizard parameter Reverse. You can hear how the two stereo sides swap positions. The ›effect‹ works as it should. Any plug-in that process the two sides independently and then puts out a stereo signal will always be a stereo in/out plug-in.

Unfortunately, the Vst Macintosh stereo in/out plug-ins either have a display function (Scopion), or they manipulate the actual stereo soundscape (Wizard). Here we're trying to show you how a stereo In-Out plug-in generates an effect without warping the stereo aspect of a signal, so these plug-ins are relatively unsuitable for demonstration purposes.

Although it might seem like blasphemy to some Macintosh meisters, I borrowed a cup of stereo from Vst Windows. It comes complete with an effect called the Grungelizer, a true stereo in/out plug-in for ›artificial audio alterations.‹ In Cd Example 19 you can hear the stereo left/right test file as manipulated by the Grungelizer (courtesy of Vst Windows) installed in the Insert rack.

◎ **19**—This is what a true stereo plug-in sounds like: Both sides are processed but their stereo positions remain intact.

Mono In/Stereo Out

1 Open Example Song 20. Here the plug-in Stereo Echo is active in the Insert rack of the stereo channel. You can hear that the left channel is being processed, the right side of the dry signal has disappeared altogether. This is conclusive evidence that you're dealing with a plug-in that is equipped with a mono input.

2 Open the Master channel and note that the left and right Led chain respond differently. This discrepancy is due to the spatial characteristics of the effects signal.

3 Press the Mono button. You can hear the delay signal ›collapse.‹ You can use the button to check our more subtle effects such as reverb to see if a stereo signal is generated.

◎ **20**—This is how a Mono In/Stereo Out effect works in the Stereo Insert: The left channel is processed, the right is muted. The different delays on the two sides indicate that the effect is indeed stereo.

Mono In/Out

1 Now select the plug-in ›Electro Fuzz‹ as the Insert effect. Caution, this little beast cranks out some serious gain. Unless you want to hear hells' bells for the next couple of days, turn the Volume and Boost parameters down to minimal settings.

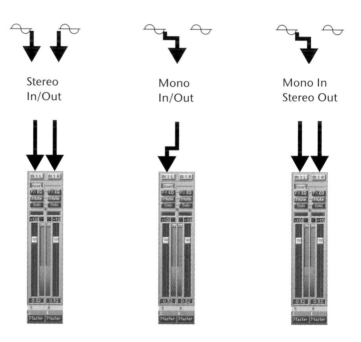

21—This is how a Mono in/out effect works in the Stereo Insert: Here too only the left channel is processed. However, when you switch to mono, you won't hear any difference in the effects signal.

2 Here too you can hear that only the left channel is processed: Ergo, the plug-in features a mono input.

3 When you try out the LED test in the Master section, you can see that both LED chains are totally in sync when ›Left‹ is spoken. This and the mono listening test tells you that the effects signal of the Electro Fuzz is routed out in mono only.

Electro Fuzz puts out a mono effects signal in parallel to two output circuits, which is why you hear the signal dead-center of the soundscape. Some plug-ins by third-party vendors are limited to a single output (see the diagrams on page 113). With this type of plug-in, you will hear the effects signal on the left side only.

▶ Distinguishing between a Mono In/Out and Mono In/Stereo Out plug-in is more a matter of micromanagement than anything else—in practice, the difference isn't all that important. On the other hand, you definitely need to establish if you are dealing with mono or stereo in plug-in to prevent undesirable side-effects!

Signal routing via effects inserts in a stereo channel depends on the type of plug-in that you're using and is thus not easy to discern.

Stereo In/Out

Mono In/Out

Mono In Stereo Out

Use the stereo test file to find out how Send rack works. While you're at it, play around with internal level parameters of the plug-ins.

▶ Occasionally, moving the stereo channel faders individually can be an edifying experience. Press and hold the ⌥ key on your computer keyboard to divorce the two faders when you are attempting this feat. The faders of a stereo channel in VST are normally married automatically.

Optimizing Effects Levels

When you're routing signals to plug-ins, it is essential that you dial in an appropriate signal level. None of the VST effects devices are equipped with knobs to control the effect signal's output level or the effects balance. You have the following alternatives for determining the extent of an effect's influence:

Effects Input

You can control the effect's output level by reducing the level of the signal that you are routing to its input. The exceptions to this rule are special plug-ins that generate signals internally. When you are routing signals via Send, you can use the Send knobs to determine the level for individual channels, or you can control signal levels globally via the Effects Master knob. Many plug-ins also feature internal input gain controls.

Effects Output

In the majority of effects plug-ins, you'll find an internal parameter that lets you control the effects output level. In the VST plug-ins, which are edited via the control elements of the virtual effects devices, you will always find these controls on the last parameter page (Out Levl).

Effects Balance

Manipulating the effects input and output signal level via the plug-in's internal controls is a sensible option only when you are using a Send circuit. When you are using an Insert signal routing setup, the entire signal is patched through the effect, so you would also be influencing the level of the dry signal. In most cases, you will prefer to control the dry signal level via the channel fader.

For this reason, many plug-ins feature a parameter called ›Effects Balance‹ or simply ›Mix.‹ This internal plug-in control lets you determine the balance between (or mix of) the direct (dry) and effects (wet) signals.

Generally you will use an Insert effect to bend the entire signal (i. e. 100 % effect), but there are exceptions. This is precisely why I have to express the rare complaint: It's a crying shame that VST's internal plug-ins do not feature a control for the effects balance.

When you are using an Insert, this parameter is the only tool that you have at your disposal for variably determining the relationship between the wet and dry signals.

The situation is entirely different with the Send routing option. If you are using a third-party vendor's plug-in that is equipped with an effects balance knob, you should always set it to maximum effect (100 % Wet). Otherwise you will end up hearing the dry signal twice: Once via the channel circuit and once via the effects output circuit. If you're unaware of what's causing the duplicate signal, you will end up questioning your sanity! What's more, it will cause all kinds of technical problems such as runtime discrepancies, phase cancellations and comb filtering effects which can lead to a washed-out, indistinct sound.

The Right Level

When you are using the Send effects signal routing circuit, you should ensure that the input and output signals are balanced properly so that you don't encounter undesirable side-effects:

♦ If the output level of the plug-in is set too low internally, you will have to turn the input well up so that you can hear the effect with the desired intensity. This may lead to digital distortion within the plug-in that you won't necessarily see, but certainly will hear.

◆ If the output level of the plug-in is set too high internally, you will have to turn the input well down so the effect isn't too loud.

This can cause problems in plug-ins where the algorithms emulate analog equipment. To generate effects, these plug-ins' computations are based on a specific level that is equivalent to the ideal input level.

On the other hand, in some recording situations you might find that these ›wanton‹ settings suddenly make sense, for example when the internal control range of a plug-in isn't what you would like it to be (see ›Electro Fuzz‹ on page 126).

As complicated as all of this sounds, there's no reason to be intimidated. You'll find that in practical applications, you'll soon get the hang of balancing the levels of plug-ins. The majority of these are designed rather well; they'll respond properly to a fairly wide range of levels.

Just avoid going overboard, and you'll be good to go. Definitely do not go the Nigel Tufnel route and set all level knobs to 11 in a Send routing setup. Try level values of 70 to 80 % of maximum and fine-tune the settings from there for the best results. This method will produce good results much faster than any manic knob-twiddling exercises.

6 Internal Vsт Plug-ins

The option of purchasing and adding plug-ins to your arsenal of internal effects is pretty nifty. Although your account manager might not be as pleased as you are, this possibility is exactly what makes this system flexible enough to match your evolving tastes.

The popularity of the software has cultivated a vast range of Vsт-compatible effects plug-ins. The list of available products is staggering, which is why in this book I've limited my comments to the internal Vsт effects plug-ins.

On the CD-Rom included with this book, you'll find a folder that features a bunch of freeware and shareware plug-ins; its a complimentary preview of the Wizoo Guide Vsт Plug-Ins (refer to the catalog at the end of the book). Feel free to use these to expand your Vsт effects rack (see page 176).

In the chapter on Eqs, you read about a method that lets you enter graphical parameter values more precisely. You should use the same method for editing effects parameters. You don't have to call up the Alpha Dial first. Simply click on the effects parameter, drag the mouse cursor to the edge of the screen and move it along the border of the window. You can also click on the parameter while holding the ⌘ key down and changing the parameter by moving the mouse vertically.

Plug-ins with Mono Input

Most of the Vsт standard plug-ins are equipped with a mono input. You can use these in the Insert racks and Send Effects rack, but not in the Master Effects rack.

Auto Pan

This is a plug-in featuring a mono input and a stereo output. It lets you sweep signals back and forth between speakers. Auto Pan does what it should, but no more than that.

One of my biggest gripes is that you can't set the modulation rate so that it matches the song tempo. If you want to pan a signal to the beat of your music, don't expect Auto Pan to do the trick, draw the requisite panorama automation data in the Audio Editor instead. More on this in the section ›Automation and Effects‹ on page 154.

If you want to use Auto Pan for a gentle sweep, definitely select the Sine Lғo waveshape. Everything else will generate a kind of skip which—depending on the audio material—will be audible, much like the sound of a broken record.

The Sine waveshape is great for generating effects similar to tremolo for guitars or electric pianos. All you have to do is route the effect out in mono:

22—An unadulterated guitar line.

1   Place Auto Pan as an Insert effect for the mono channel.

2   In Auto Pan, select the waveshape Sine, set the Width value and Lғo rate as desired. The effect is inserted in a mono channel, so of course you will hear the effects output signal in mono. This reduces the sweeping effect that is audible when the panorama is reproduced in stereo to the type of shimmering volume effect generated by a tremolo.

23—Pack up the tremolo, start up the reverb and head for Twin Peaks.

3   Slap on a bit of reverb via Send and David Lynch may hire you for his next project.

Choirus and Choirus 2

No, it's not a misspelling, and yes, there are two variation of the chorus effect—›Choirus‹ and ›Choirus 2.‹ Both effects are equipped with a mono input and a stereo output. The control options not only comprise standard parameters such as delay rate, modulation depth, Lғo Frequency and feedback, but also other more unusual parameters such as Feed Bal (balance between the feedback and direct signals) and Glimmer 1 / 2 (density of the effects signal).

The first Vsт Macintosh version featured just one ›Choirus‹ algorithm. Soon users began voicing entirely justified complaints that the plug-in tends to generate digital distortion before you can say ›What an infernal noise.‹ Steinberg responded by developing the algorithm ›Choirus 2‹ and integrating it in Vsт 3.5 and higher. The original ›Choirus‹ was doomed, but a couple Beta testers managed to win a veto of the plans to scrap it. They wanted to hang on to the ›Choirus‹ as an alternative precisely because of its ›nifty distortion.‹

They got their wish and we another chorus. Now VST Macintosh ships with two remarkably similar chorus plug-ins with fundamentally different sounds.

► Use the ›Choirus‹ when you're in the mood for slumming; it adds more ›grit,‹ for example to lend a vintage flavor to sterile synthesizer Rhodes Sounds. Choirus 2 is a much cleaner effect and is thus more suitable for ›classy‹ chorus sounds.

Choirus and Choirus 2 are definitely some of the finer representatives of their breed. A common problem of digital chorus algorithms is that the effect is either totally inaudible or generates an annoying wobbly sound—these effects are free of such ills. You can use them to generate anything from modulation effects for a slighter fatter sound through to heavy-duty sci-fi sounds. You can also generate self-resonance to create truly warped effects:

1 Insert one of the two Choirus effects to the mono channel and set the parameters Feed Balance and Feedback to relatively high values.
2 What you're hearing is self-resonance which you can use to bend any vocal so that it sounds robotic.
3 Vary the Time parameter and the LFO frequency.

24—A ›normal‹ voice sample.

25—Attack of the Zylones—self-resonance through chorus feedback.

You can also apply this method to percussion and drum signals to achieve interesting results.

Espacial

The original VST reverb also features a mono input and a stereo output. When you consider its miserly performance requirements, it delivers good effects quality. The newer Wunderverb 3 however puts it to shame. The problem with Espacial is its lack of high end dampening. Consequently, the reverb sounds brittle and a bit harsh.

If you've got a thing for natural-sounding reverb, go for the WunderVerb 3. Nevertheless, Steinberg shouldn't oust Espacial from VST because it is more flexible in terms of early reflections and thus suitable for creating special percussion rooms that WunderVerb 3 can't manage.

For percussion and drums, usually smaller rooms with brief delays will sound better. Otherwise the delay between the dry and wet signals will be too great and you'll end up with an indirect sound and ambiguous timing.

In contrast to high-end reverb devices and plug-ins, Espacial is not an intelligent virtual device. This doesn't mean that it's a bit slow on the uptake, only that the parameters do not interact—i. e. influence each other. If you're unfamiliar with basic acoustics and unaware of how parameters interact, it won't take much for simulated rooms to end up with an unnatural sound.

You should keep two basic rules in mind when you are going for natural-sounding rooms:

◆ In the real world, a large room (Page 1: Size) usually generates a lengthier reverberation (Page 1: Time). The Espacial algorithm's relatively modest high end damping of the reverb part of the signal imitates this quite accurately.

◆ The pre-delay time that elapses prior to the early reflection (Page 2: Er Start)—in other words, the attack time—has a strong influence on how our ears perceive the size of a room. If you're trying to create the impression of a larger room, you should definitely keep this parameter in mind.

Electro Fuzz

Click on the round button at the bottom center of the plug-in to open a condensed online help.

Electro Fuzz is equipped with a mono input and output and is limited to three parameters.

◆ Boost controls the amount of gain and thus the degree of distortion. If you turn this control up but want the level to remain constant, you'll have to turn the Volume parameter down to balance out the increase in level.

◆ Clipback inverts the upper portion of the generated wave-shape; this creates more overtones for an opener, harsher and more aggressive sound.

▶ Don't expect amp simulation from the Electro Fuzz, it is unabashedly synthetic. If you plug an electric guitar directly into the mixer, you won't enjoy the benefit of a warm, harmonically complex overdriven sound that a good tube amp or more sophisticated plug-in will produce.

Electro Fuzz is fine for roughing up the smooth edges of drums, percussion or organs. The Mono in/out circuit of the plug-in won't do for stereo material, so you'll have to use two Send effects circuits with separate Electro Fuzz plug-ins.

There is a setting that will generate a rather subtle, warm sound that isn't immediately identifiable as distortion but nevertheless adds some dirt to the signal. This setting will spice up many types of sounds.

1 Route the signal to the Electro Fuzz via the Post-Fader Send mode and turn the effects send knob and the effects input to about a third of the way up.

◎ **26**—A synth line that could do with a bit of sprucing up without going the headbanger route.

2 Set Boost To a middle value (around 40) and Volume to an extremely low value so that a subtle effect is generated.

3 Set Clipback to 0 for more warmth.

4 At high Volume and low Boost values, primarily the signal peaks are distorted. In our example, this doesn't sound revelatory, but if you try it with other audio material, you'll find you can up with some fairly interesting stuff.

◎ **27**—Everything (well, almost) sounds more interesting with a dab of distortion.

Try out these types of subtle grit-enhancing maneuvers with vocals. Here less is definitely more, but with a light touch and a dash of Electro Fuzz voodoo, you will be able to lend a track or two a bit more charisma.

Stereo Echo

It's all in the name, but only in terms of the output. The input of this plug-in is mono. On three pages, it offers access to delay time, feedback and level—all separately for the left and

right stereo channel. Delay 1 normally addresses the left stereo out, Delay 2 the right. The maximum delay time is 500
ms in stereo.

If you find that you want or need to, you can use the parameter with the somewhat confusing name Del2 Balance to
route the output of Delay 2 to the input of Delay 1, a process
that in audio engineering jargon is called cross-delay, which
has absolutely nothing to do with cross-dressing. If you set
the parameter to the maximum value of 1.0, Delay 1 receives
the output signal of Delay 2, along with the normal left input
signal. This signal routing option lets you come up with more
complex stereo effects.

You can also link the two channels via the accurately
named Link parameter. The delay then operates in mono
output mode and only the settings for Delay 1 take effect. The
maximum delay time is doubled to a total length of one second, so you can attend to other important stuff like doing
your taxes while you're waiting for the echo to return.

▶ In addition to the exceptionally coarse resolution of the delay times,
another flaw of this plug-in is that it does not feature an option that
lets you set delay times based on tempo. This makes it hard to generate rhythmic echo effects. Use Dave Brown's freeware plug-in ›Tempo
Delay‹ on the Cd-Rom instead.

Delays such as this one are good for more than imitating the
ubiquitous call of the mountain man. You can also generate
experimental tonal coloration, for instance to add a synthetic
touch to drums or percussion or a bit more spatial depth:

28—A conga groove
that may sound too natural
for true sound blasters.

1 Route the signal to the Stereo Echo via Post-Fader Send.

2 Work with medium Feedback values and, for the sake of simplicity,
link the two delay circuits (Link On) for now. Set Delay 1 to times in
the 5 to 40 ms range.

29—The result doesn't
sound much like an echo,
but weirdness is good too.

3 Switch Link to Off and assign the other Delay a different time within
the range mentioned above to generate a more complex sound. Use a
cross-delay (Del2 Bal set to medium to high values) to add even more
spice to the generated comb filtering effects.

▶ **Caution:** When you are messing around with these types of experiments, keep one hand on the volume control of the mixer or monitor. If the Feedback parameter is set to too high a value, the signal may build up to an endless loop, which leads to a rapid increase in level and ultimately distortion. Your computer won't be fazed at all, but your monitor system and your ears may never forgive you.

WunderVerb 3

WunderVerb features a mono in and a stereo out. Its parameters are limited to the bare essentials: room Size, Decay and Damp, which puts a damper on the highs. The only parameter that you may actually miss is a much-coveted effects level control. You'll just have to make do with manipulating the Send input signal.

Wonder indeed, I know of no other reverb plug-in that comes even close to delivering this level of effects quality on as little Cpu power. WunderVerb 3 requires half the computing performance of Vst's Espacial, which is pretty darn impressive when you consider that Espacial doesn't exactly wolf down on resources.

Although WunderVerb 3 has substantially fewer parameter than its spacey cousin, it has a considerable advantage over Espacial: A high frequency damping feature, the Damp parameter. In most cases, this feature will let you come up with more natural, unobtrusive reverberation than you could with Espacial.

WunderVerb3 is great for lengthy, smooth reverberations typical of balladesque piano, sax, vocals or strings sounds. Espacial—with its intricately variable early reflection—on the other hand is suited to drums and percussion.

▶ When you're working with solo signals (a capella vocals, etc.) you may detect a phenomenon particular to the WunderVerb: It leaves a gap in the middle of the stereo field and instead emphasizes the sides. This type of flanking maneuver might be great in cavalry battle, but in the context of your music, you might find it less appealing. If you can't live with the hole that leads to nowhere, try the Espacial; its stereo image is a bit more balanced.

▶ Even if the quality of WunderVerb 3 doesn't meet your standards for final mixdown and you prefer to use a high-end reverb such as Waves TrueVerb, you should still use WunderVerb 3 while you are composing and arranging. It will do just fine as a stand-in for your ultimate reverb, especially when you consider that you will have a great deal more performance power available while you're working. You'll be able to knock out all of the tasks leading up to mixdown much quicker and in greater comfort.

Tun-a

Apart from its fishy name, this ›virtual tuner‹ has the look and feel of a chromatic tuning device. Tun-a is a stripped-down version of a plug-in that Steinberg initially released for the TDM platform. The functions in the VST Macintosh version are only a tad less sophisticated and you get it for free, so no calls for complaints here.

A fader lets you select diverse classical scales. The default status here is Equal, which is equivalent to the tuning of contemporary keyboards. Incoming notes are automatically analyzed. The plug-in displays the note name and octave as copy text. A scale indicates deviations from the ›ideal‹ tuning.

A tone generator is also integrated; it produces a test tone with variable pitch, octave and tuning.

► Although the parameter for the frequency of concert-pitch A is displayed above the section for the test tone, it doesn't just influence the tone generator, but also the tuning devices' analysis function. By varying this parameter, you can ›calibrate‹ the Tun-a. Dead-center of the value range lies at 440 Hz, considered standard for pop music. You can vary this value by 20 Hz in either direction.

The plug-in is fast and precise. You can rely on its analysis and thus retire your external tuning device.

The only drawback: This version of the Tun-a features just a mono input. You can't drop it in the Master effects rack, which in my humble opinion would be the most practical place for it to be.

Plug-ins with Stereo Inputs

And now on to a rare breed in VST Macintosh—plug-ins with stereo inputs. Here the Tun-a problem is just the opposite: You can install these to the Master Effects rack only, not to the Send Effects rack.

Scopion

Scopion is a master plug-in which predestines it for true stereo—i.e. it is equipped with a stereo input and output. This accurate emulation of a vintage oscilloscope features a lever that lets you select the left or right channel for display. Two knobs are located at the bottom. One knob influences the amplitude, i.e. the vertical spread of the display. The other varies the sampling frequency, i.e. the horizontal spread of the displayed time window.

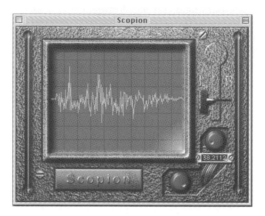

Scopion is a cute little toy, but won't do you much good when you're attempting to get some ›serious‹ work done in VST. Here's the obligatory exception to the rule: This plug-in is a good optical sensor which you can use to detect the latency of your system (see page 58):

◆ If latency is low, you won't perceive any delay—as soon as you see the oscilloscope pulsate, you'll hear the corresponding signal.

◆ When latency is high, you'll see the oscilloscope pulsate well before you hear the signal.

Use the Scopion when you are trying out audio card drivers.

Wizard

This stereo in/out plug-in is limited to two parameters. The Wizard lets you swap the left and right stereo channel. The actual effect becomes audible when you turn up the Amount parameter. It shifts the phase, which has the aural effect of expanding the stereoscopic image.

Any time you process a signal via phase shifting, you should be very cautious. This type of manipulation decreases mono compatibility—the mixdown sounds different when it is piped through a mono system. The relationship between the volume levels of individual signals shifts depending on if the individual signals were recorded in stereo or mono.

The balance between the dry and wet signals also changes. A mono piano with a stereo reverb sounds roomier after the Wizard has worked its wizardry because the phase shift boosts stereo signals while cutting mono signals.

Use the Wizard only when you want to fix something in the finished mix that you can no longer access via any other means. When you're mixing down your own recordings, you will have access to all of the individual components of the master signal, so you generally won't need the Wizard.

When you use this plug-in, ensure you check out the result over a mono circuit (Mono button in the Master section). Also listen to the result via headphones, this way you will be able to hear undesirable side-effects of a stereo manipulation even more clearly.

Externalizer

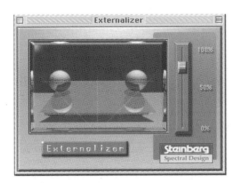

Finally, a virtual out-of-body experience. Seriously though, this stereo in/out plug-in is designed to optimize a stereo signal for headphones playback. The concept is that the typical localization of signals that you experience in your head when you're wearing headphones is altered to simulate the soundscape as perceived through speakers—pyschoacoustically out of your head indeed.

Obviously, the designers put a lot of effort in the visuals of this plug-in. Its control parameters are limited to one: Effect Intensity. When you crank it up, the ›virtual position‹ of the signal indeed changes. The sonic landscape is shifted from the headphones-typical central position; the signal seems to be coming from a position that is both higher and further forward, which does alter your in-head perception. However, the space of the stereo signal is also compressed somewhat: Everything seems tighter and the panorama less spacious.

▶ Psychoacoustic algorithms that manipulate spacial localization usually work with level or phase manipulations in defined frequency ranges. The Externalizer algorithm does not alter the balance between the mono and stereo components as radically as the simplistic phase shifting effect of the Wizard. However, at extreme settings, it changes the frequency response of the audio material: The signal sounds colored or filtered. These side-effects are particularly prominent when you reduce the signal to mono.

Although it's an interesting toy, the Externalizer is really only practical if you want to prep a recording specifically for playback via headphones. Whether or not this effect is actually worth the trade-off—you will have to cope with undesirable side-effects—can only be judged on a case-by-case basis and certainly depends on the type of material that you're dealing with. My recommendation is that I don't have one: It's entirely up to you if you choose to use it.

▶ Always check psychoacoustic ›add-on effects‹ carefully for undesirable side-effects. No matter how cool an effect seems in isolated detail, it won't be worth it if you have to sacrifice the quality of the overall signal for it.

7 Where and with What Can You Use Automation?

Vst features two types of automation processes: so-called ›dynamic events‹ and the automation function in the Vst mixer.

▶ Depending on system latency (see page 59), you will encounter delay between automation data and audio data in Vst. This effect would adulterate the audio examples, so I was compelled to present these results in the form of fully computed audio files, which I created using Track Bouncing. Definitely attempt to copy these results; guided by the descriptions and illustrations, you should be able to come up with something similar to my finished audio file.

Using Dynamic Events

You can automate volume and panorama via dynamic events. The advantage of this method is that control data is integrated in the audio regions. Consequently, when the regions are shifted to another location, control data remain exactly where you want them to be.

Dynamic events are great for effects such as fades or panning, where you want to hear the effect but don't want to edit the actual audio file.

The majority of application options for dynamic events are fairly clear-cut. They're great for stuff like non-destructive fade in/outs or muting mic noises during pauses.

There is however a nifty application for dynamic volume events that is not apparent at first glance. It comes in handy if you don't own a special compressor plug-in:

Compressor Function

A typical characteristic of uncompressed signals is that they often have just a few loud signal peaks that push at the threshold of the maximum allowable dynamic range. A compressor irons out precisely these peaks so that you end up with a ›smooth‹ signal, in other words, a signal with less drastic level deviations. This lets you tweak the entire signal so that it sounds tighter and punchier.

You can emulate this type of compression via dynamic volume events:

30—Too much of a good thing: An overly dynamic, uncompressed vocal track.

1   Double-click on the vocal segment to open the Lane Editor. Select the item Dynamic Events from the local View menu, then the item Volume from the menu in the middle, and under S (Snap), the entry Off so that you can move the dots freely.

2   Select the pencil via the right mouse button. Press and hold the ⌨ key and click on the Volume line located under the waveshape to draw new dots. Release the ⌨ key. You can now re-position the dots to shape a control curve.

3   Use the waveshape display to locate the words that are too loud (in this case, those in the central region), and lower the volume with the help of the control curve as depicted in the diagram.

4   Ensure that you set the dots to positions where the signal pauses. If the steps are audible, use short lines drawn at angles instead.

5   Listen closely to the results and reposition the dots so the reduction in levels sounds unobtrusive.

▶ Depending on latency (see page 58), there is a delay between the visual display of the waveshape and audio output. This of course changes the relationship to control data such as dynamic events. If the delay is prominent, you can't rely fully on the waveshape, you'll have to do it by ear, i.e. listen closely and reposition the dots until the results sound good.

31—After editing, the level is more streamlined.

Check out Track 2 in the audio file. Here you'll find an example of the kind of results that this method will let you come up with. First I lowered the overly loud passage in the middle of the vocal file in the same manner as described above. Then the result was exported to Track 2 via track bouncing and brought up to maximum level via the function Normalize in the Vst Wave Editor.

The resulting signal is more compact and thus stands out better in the mix.

▶ This method does take some time, effort and patience to come up with the ideal settings. Some audio engineers insist that the manual or automated fader manipulations that this process emulates is the only way to go. The results often sound more dynamic and natural than a comparable compressor-treated passage would—provided of course you do it right.

By drawing volume control curves, you can decrease the level of overly loud passages in signals and thus achieve an effect similar to compression.

Rhythmic Panning

The Vst-internal Auto Pan plug-in does not allow you to enter parameters directly in the form of bpm. There are of course other more luxurious plug-ins, but you'll only have to shell more of your hard-earned pennies for them. Besides, the vast majority of these are limited to more or less routine audio ping-pong rather than truly programmable panning effects.

Dynamic pan events are more versatile, they let you draw exactly the type of panorama rhythm that you want.

1 Call up the dynamic events for the region, but this time activate Pan instead of Volume in the middle pop-up-menu.

2 Nothing appears? This is normal. You have to use the pencil while pressing and holding the ⌥ key to first draw at least one dot to ›de-neutralize‹ the panorama line.

(◎) **32**–A 16th synth stac-cato.

33—Just one of the many possible rhythmic panning options.

3 Use the same method described earlier to draw panorama interval ›jumps‹ (steps) or smooth sequences (angled lines). Feel free to experiment: You don't have to limit yourself to a mundane imitation of baseline tennis, go ahead and try out different non-symmetrical patterns.

Mixer Automation

It doesn't take much to learn how to operate the VST mixer automation; besides, the handbook provides an in-depth explanation. So instead of reiterating all of that stuff, we'll use this space more wisely and discuss some practical tips and example applications:

Recording Static Automation Data

VST will only acknowledge ›reasonable‹ parameters in the basic automation configuration. If for example you want to use an effect later on in the course of the song, switch it on before you press the Write button for the first time. Otherwise VST will ignore the requisite effects parameters which will later irritate you to no end.

The way automation in hardware mixing consoles works is that you first configure a static automation scene and then add the dynamic elements to the mix. You should apply the same technique to the VST mixer automation, you'll find that in most cases, this is the most practical method:

The terms ›static automation‹ refer to basic settings—usually a scene for the diverse song parts—that are switched ›hard‹ (as opposed to a gradual or gliding fade from one setting to the next). Here's how you go about creating static scenes:

1 Play back your first song part in Cycle mode and dial in the desired Channel/Group Mixer settings.

2 Stop the playback. Briefly switch the Write button in the Mixer window on and then off again. VST just generated an automation track called Audio Mix. Your entire mixer configuration is saved at Position 1.01 in this track.

3 Go to your next song part and check if you need different mixer settings. If this is indeed the case, memorize or preferably jot down the mixer parameters that you want to change from the original mix.

4 Stop the playback. Set the Song Cursor to the beginning of the second song part. For precise navigation, simply type the desired song posi-

tion to the black field on the left side of the Transport window of use the Marker function.

5   Switch the Write button on and set the Mixer parameters that you want to change to the desired positions. Ensure that you remain in Stop mode. It is also essential that you reposition every parameter that you want to change regardless of how many these might be, and that the new position is correct once you're finished.

6   Switch the Write button off again. You have just written all of the parameters for which you changed the settings to the desired song positions in an automation track.

7   Repeat Steps 3 to 6 for all song parts.

Once you're finished, you can press the read Read button to play back the entire song. VST should abruptly activate the new parameter settings at the positions that you edited.

Adding Dynamic Automation

Once you have knocked out all of the static parameter changes, you will in most cases require continuous parameter changes such as fades or panning—in other words, so-called Dynamic Automation:

1   Activate the Read and Write buttons simultaneously and play back the static automation setup that you programmed.

2   At whatever positions that you want to insert continuous parameter changes, simply ›grab‹ the corresponding control element and move it in real-time while your song is being played back. VST will only over-write a parameter's current automation data if you manipulate it during playback.

3   You can play back the song as often as you like to edit it. Once you've finished, deactivate the Write button and play back the entire automation sequence with the Read button activated.

You can overwrite and edit automation data literally forever—more on this on page 141. It won't take much to end up with a convoluted mess of data, so I recommend that you save the song every time you initiate a new editing run. If you do this, you can always fall back on the previous mix when the need arises.

If you assign a number to each intermediate mix, you can always recall a particular mix. Occasionally you'll detect a slight mistake that you made in your automation fervor much later on. In this case, the extra effort required to number the mixes pays off in spades.

The Higher Art of Automation

With the VST mixer automation, you can record volume and panorama events, among others. Consequently, you have the same type of manipulation options that you became familiar with when you were working with dynamic events (see ›Using Dynamic Events‹ from page 135 onwards).

The ›others‹ mentioned above refer to all other parameters: EQs, effects and panning. This sounds pretty exciting, and believe me, it is.

We all love to sound like we know the ins and outs of what we're doing. You can impress yourself and others by targeting specific effects and exploiting the automation function to manipulate these. Your production will sound more ›professional.‹ A good example would be for instance a lush refrain arrangement. It can certainly do with more reverb on the vocals than say a sparsely arranged verse.

Rhythmic EQ, panorama and effects manipulations can also deliver interesting results:

⊚ **34**—A drum loop, wild enough for most, but not for us.

1   Play back the loop in Cycle mode and create a couple of conspicuous EQ and effects settings.

2   Use static or dynamic automation to activate these settings rhythmically. Use primarily buttons such as EQ On/Off rather than continuous controls. This generates a lot less data, wreaks less havoc on the timing and is much easier to edit later on.

⊚ **35**—The same loop with two rhythmically automated EQ bands and a short delay.

3   Play back the automated sequence and check out the results.

Editing Automation Data in the List Editor

If you want to execute any kind of post-recording repairs, for instance to polish the rhythmic EQs, you can edit the automation track as easy as you would a MIDI track:

1 Select the Audio Mix segment and activate List in the Edit menu to open the List Editor. Here you can view all of the recorded automation events as individual entries in a list.

2 Drag the vertical partition line at the right of the test entries all the way to the right until the Comment appears. This column displays comments on each event that tells you the type of data that you're dealing with.

3 You can manipulate every event in the usual fashion, i.e. you can delete, move or quantize it.

You can also edit the automation track in the normal manner without the benefit of the list—for instance cut, copy or temporarily ›park‹ segments on another mixer tracks.

Editing Data in the Controller Editor

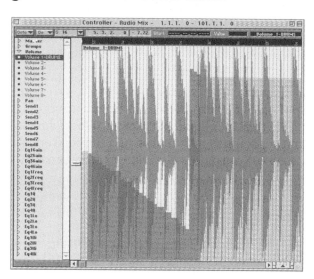

From Macintosh Version 4.0, VST offers another option for post-editing and even generating mixer automation data. Although the new Controller Editor is limited to crucial automation data (Volume for Master and Groups; Volume, Pan, Send and EQ parameters for Channel Mixer channels), it is certainly the most comfortable option for editing these select parameters:

1 Double-click on the Audio Mix segment to open it in the Controller Editor.

2 At the left, you'll see a list of the type of automation data that can be edited. Click on an entry, e.g. the Volume arrow. A submenu will appear listing all Channel Mixer channels. If the entry is preceded by a dot, this indicates that you have already generated automation data for this type of parameter, e.g. by recording it directly in the Mixer.

3 For example if you select Volume 1, the waveshape of the Audio Region on Track 1 will appear. If you have already recorded Volume control data, the waveshape will be shaded in green.

4 The diverse tools let you comfortably edit automation data: The normal mouse cursor selects the region; the fader to the left of the data window lets you scale the automation data. The cross allows you to draw the scaling curve directly. Press and hold the 🔄 key to use the pencil to draw automation data freehand.

5 Check out the local Do menu. There you'll find interesting functions for editing selected regions, e.g. automatic smoothing (Smooth).

▶ As in all Vst editors, the local S menu (Snap) determines the maximum resolution of the data sequence as a function of time. Keep in mind that at the finest resolution (Off), loads of automation data is generated, which is hardly advantageous to Vst timing.

The Controller Editor's comfortable user interface makes it your first choice when you want to edit or draw automation data. You should only use the methods (dynamic events, editing in the List Editor) described in other sections only if there is a compelling reason to do so.

8 The Miracle Worker: Track Bouncing

The name that Steinberg gave Vsт's Track Bouncing is an unintentional understatement—they should have called something like Dr. Vsт's Cure-all for Recurring Resource Problems. Whenever you run out of audio tracks, effects circuits, plug-ins or Cpu power, Track Bouncing will cure your ills. Curiously, this powerful tool hides behind an unassuming little button. Don't overlook it, this feature is a life-saver (virtually, that is).

Exporting Audio Files

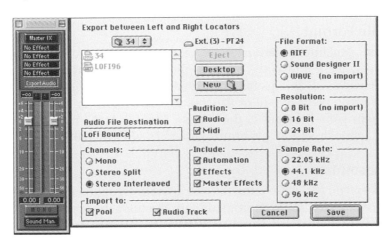

This function is easily explained.

With track bouncing, you can take the Vsт mixer's master signal

◆ and export it as an audio file and do what ever comes to mind, for instance edit it in a sample editor,

◆ or internally bounce (finally, the mystery of the name's origins are unveiled) it to a mono or stereo track.

Picture the whole process as recording via an excellent virtual tape recorder. The result is equivalent to a finished tape.

The essential factor here is the magic word, ›digital.‹ It means that the whole process is executed without the help of DA or AD conversion, which in turn relegates signal degradation to a nominal figure. The method is simple:

1   Use locators to ›fence in‹ the segment that you want to export.

2   Click on the Export Audio button in the master section or select the menu item Export Audio Tracks from the File menu.

3   Enter the destination and a file name—confirm via OK.

Here are a few tips on the parameters that will help you to identify the right export format for your purpose:

File Format

VST Macintosh features the export formats AIFF, Sound Designer II and Wave. Wave is the preferred format for Windows PC, SD II is usually reserved for the Macintosh.

If you want to edit or process the file further in VST Macintosh, your best bet is the ›house format‹ AIFF—many other Macintosh and PC programs can work with this format.

Resolution

Here you can determine the word width for audio data: 8 bits are fine for most multimedia productions because for this type of application you usually want to keep the audio files as small as possible. 24 bits is a sensible option for DVD mastering or editing in a computer that enables import of this format (or if you use ›VST/24,‹ see page 19). 16 bits are the contemporary standard for the CD audio format, so in most cases this will be your best choice.

Sample Rate

◆ 22.05 kHz is suitable for multimedia applications, where minimum memory requirements have priority over sound quality. Often, you'll need 11.025 kHz, but unfortunately nobody told Steinberg: VST doesn't feature this option.

◆ 48 kHz is recommended for video post-production applications only.

◆ Contemporary CD audio uses 44.1 kHz, and this is usually your best bet.

▶ All other sample rates have to be converted when you want to produce a master CD. This type of conversion degrades the signal, which needless to say is undesirable.

◆ In VST/24, you can also select 96 kHz, provided you own the requisite audio hardware. If you do own this type of high-end system, you'll presumably have invested for a specific purpose. The standard application here is of course DVD mastering.

Channels

It's entirely up to whether you want to generate a mono or a stereo file. If you do choose stereo, which type of stereo is best?

Stereo Split actually consists of two separate mono files, Stereo Interleaved is a stereo file.

◆ Stereo Split means that the respective right and left channels are saved as separate files. VST conveniently attaches an L or R to the file name to identify the channel.

You should only use this format when the post-production process that you want to torment these files with calls for it. If you want to use an audio editor or CD burner software that can't open any other format, the point is moot. Another application that Stereo Split is good for is when you have recorded two different microphone signals to a stereo track and want to edit these separately.

◆ In Stereo Interleaved mode, the two stereo sides are interwoven into a single file. If there aren't any compelling reasons not to, you should use this format for Vst Macintosh.

Import

If both fields are suddenly shaded gray, then Vst cannot import the selected format. Check out the settings for File Format and Resolution and change them if necessary.

The Import To field lets you save a file and simultaneously import it to the current Song (Pool) or even directly to an Audio Track.

We used this technique for some of the following Cd examples. Select an available audio track before you activate the Export Audio function. Then activate both options mentioned above. The formats for the destination track and the file that you want to generate of course have to be identical (mono/stereo).

▶ The major advantage of direct import is that the new file automatically ends up exactly in the right position.

Lightening the Cpu's Load

If you've already worked with Vst and a Macintosh that's been around for a while, you'll be all too familiar with this situation: You need more tracks, but your obstinate computer won't give them up.

Combining Tracks

You can outsmart your stubborn box by combining tracks via track bouncing:

1 Mix the tracks to achieve the best possible results in terms of Eqs, level and panorama.

2 Call up track bouncing and simultaneously import the tracks to one or two available audio tracks.

3 Delete the original tracks from the arrangement (but not under any circumstances the files from the disk!).

Be aware that you no longer have discrete access to levels and dry/wet signal balance in the individual tracks. If you need different effects or a common effect with different levels for the diverse signals, you should incorporate these effects in the track bouncing procedure.

Computing in Effects and Automation

Letting the processor compute effects into track bouncing when you are combining tracks is a nifty option, but you can exploit this function to solve another problem: Say you want to slap more effects on your mix, but the Cpu has long since tossed in the towel. Yep, you guessed it, track bouncing will grease those processing skids. Not only is this a great way to free up plug-ins, you can also go the whole hog and capture parallel or serial effects combinations or automation in your audio files so that generations to come can marvel at your genius.

If your computer is too stubborn to go along for the ride when you want to activate all effects simultaneously, you can of course break the process down into individual steps. With a little patience and perseverance, any desired combination of parallel and serial effects is also possible.

Recording Effect Signals Separately

If you're heading for a bottleneck in Cpu performance for plug-ins but still have enough audio tracks available, you can also record pure effects signals, i. e. independently from the dry signal. This method is only suitable for add-on effects such as reverb or delay which are normally addressed via a send circuit. Although limited to these effects, this option is the more flexible alternative.

Depending on the situation, you can record a discrete effects signal for each original signal or one effect for several original signals. The important thing is that you hear the wet signal without any dry signal content and record it via Export Audio. The best way of coming up with a suitable configuration is to pull the faders for the dry signals all the way down and manipulate the effect via the Pre-fader Send knob (see ›Pre- and Post-Fader Mode‹ on page 100):

36—A snare with a reverb flag recorded separately.

◆ Try to record other separate mono or effects signals for the snare via track bouncing. Ensure the Import function is activated.

◆ Now we can get to down to manipulating the signal.

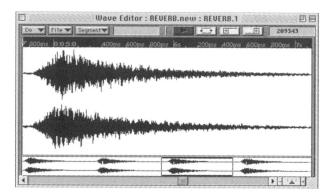

One of the neat aspects of this method is that the effects signal is now a standard audio file. Obviously, you can do all kinds of stuff with the signal in this format that you couldn't if it were just the output signal of an effects plug-in.

1 Open the reverb track in the Wave Editor by clicking on the desired Audio Region twice and again double-clicking on the waveshape in the Lane Editor after it appears.

2 Select the decay phase of the first reverb flag (approx. 2/3) and cut it off via the Silence function in the local Do menu.

3 Select the section prior to the cut and soften the hard cut via the Fade Out function.

4 Do the same thing to the remaining three reverb samples.

5 There you have it: A gated reverb that you couldn't create via an internal VST plug-in.

37—A DIY Gate Reverb.

While we're on the subject:

1 Open the Gate Reverb track in the Wave-Editor.

2 Select the entire file via ⌘Ⓐ and invert it by activating Reverse in the Do menu.

3 Play it back. Sounds ridiculous? I agree, but hang on in there...

4   Move the reverb track forward just a tad in the Arrange or Lane win-
     dow, but first switch the Snap function (S menu) to Off. Keep shifting
     the track ever so slightly until the loudest peak in the reverb track
     coincides with the attack of the original snare track.

5   Now add a bit of normal reverb to the original snare and presto, there
     you have your reverse reverb.

⊚ **38**—The only method of creating a reverse reverb effect (in this case with a snare) in VST.

This technique—recording effects signals separately—gives
you another option. You can create the audio equivalent of a
Chinese box puzzle consisting of one effect on top of another
on top of another ad infinitum. Simply record an effect, route
it through another, record the result, route it through the
next effect ... you catch my basic drift.

This technique is not as esoteric as it sounds—you can use
it for fairly ›worldly‹ applications:

1   For the vocals, record a rhythmically ›correct‹ delay to a separate track
     via Track Bouncing import.

⊚ **39**—Break out the incense: Vocals and lead chords without condiments.

2   Pull the fader for the delay track all the way down and route the signal
     via Pre-Fader Send to a reverb effect. Now the delay effect is masked
     somewhat by reverb.

3   Install a second reverb device to the Send Effects rack. Route the origi-
     nal vocal track to it via Post-Fader Send mode.

4   Carefully balance the two effects signals out until you come up with
     satisfactory results.

The good old ›delay-behind-reverb‹ combination is a popular
trick that sneaky knob twiddlers use for ballads. For this
example, we selected a sparse arrangement so that you have
to use delay/reverb sparingly; you don't want the effect to
become obtrusive. In lush arrangements, feel free to slap on
globs of ›space‹ to achieve a mightier sound.

⊚ **40**—Vocals with a blend of ›normal‹ reverb and a subtle delay, slightly masked by the second reverb.

Enough preliminaries, time to get creative.

◆   Combine a snare with the reverb flag of another snare.

◆   Pipe the signal through effects.

◆   Send the results through the Eq and automation grinder.

Even without additional plug-ins, VST offers a vast range of
sound-manipulating options.

Exporting the Final Mix to Cd

Here's a helpful hint when you're mastering: The majority of Cd players' don't track all that accurately. You shouldn't cut your Cd audio files too close to the bone. If you leave some 100 to 150 milliseconds as an intro and outro to your songs, Cd players won't Bonzai your masterpieces.

Exporting digital stereo files for Cd mastering is of course one of the most common track bouncing applications. Normally for post-production, you will require a special audio editor such as Bias Peak. However, for less ambitious projects, you can come up with decent results without an external audio editor:

1   If Midi sound generators contribute to your song, record their output signals as audio Signals. If at all possible dedicate a mono or stereo audio track to each Midi sound. If you're hard-pressed for tracks, record a stereo mix of all Midi signals to a stereo audio track and mix the ›Midi audio‹ track so that it fits in with the rest of your mixdown.

2   Don't start the song directly on the downbeat of the first bar—leave a little space before and after your song. Place the left Cursor one bar prior to the start of the song, the right Cursor one bar after the last signal fades out.

3   Use Export Audio to generate a stereo file for the entire mixdown.

4   Now we'll polish your work: Import the master that you just generated to the current or a new song and open it in the Wave Editor.

5   Select the entire file via ⌘Ⓐ and Normalize it to 0dB to bring the file up to maximum level.

6   Select the intro preceding the first signal and repeatedly apply Silence to erase any noise that may be on the track. Follow the same procedure for the outro at the end of the track. If desirable, you can first use Fade Out to mix in a clean fade-out.

7   Now we'll get down to actually fine-tuning the song: Select the entire file. Here you don't want to include the intro/outro at the beginning and end of the song. However, don't select limits that are too close, leave some 100 milliseconds before and after using the visible waveshape for orientation purposes.

8   Select the item Selection To File from the File menu and save the selected sequence as a new audio file.

The result is a normalized, final cut of a Cd audio master file. With a Cd-R recorder and the requisite software, you can burn the song directly onto an audio Cd, sell millions of copies and thank me at the Grammy awards ceremony.

Track Bouncing Stumbling Blocks

Although track bouncing is fairly straightforward, you may encounter a few virtual ›stumbling blocks‹ that are at least initially easy to overlook:

Sample Rate

If you eventually want to commit your masterpieces to CD (don't we all?), you should work in the recommended audio format in VST from the start: 16 bits and 44.1 kHz.

Any ›morning after‹ format conversion for audio export leads to roundoff error and digital filtering, which translates into signal degradation. Converting a 44.1 kHz recording upwards to 48 kHz makes no sense whatsoever, because due to roundoff error, your material will most likely end up sounding worse. Besides, this format is incompatible with the medium that the material is destined for, an audio CD.

Phase Synchronization

If you record effects separately of the dry signal, keep in mind that the original signal and the effects signal are no longer linked. If you cut or shift one of the two components, be absolutely sure that you do the same thing to the other. Pay very close attention to ensure that the timing of the two signals is identical—in other words, that you relocate both signals to precisely the same position.

If you shift a reverb track so that it deviates by only a few milliseconds from the dry signal, the spatial image will change markedly. To avoid this situation, you should hold back on this type of editing until you are in the final phase of production, when you are absolutely certain that the arrangement will remain as it is.

Reverb and Delay Flags

When you are adding reverb or delay effects, ensure you set the right Locator so that the decay phase of the effects signal is not cut off. This is why the right Locator has to be set further to the right than the immediate end of the original files. When in doubt, it's preferable to leave too much space rather than too little.

Automation and Effects

If the tracks that you want to bounce feature effects and automation, ensure that the corresponding Export parameters are activated (Include: Automation, Effects, Master Effects). If you can't hear an effect that you were intending to include in the exported file, the problem is usually due to inactive Export parameters.

Peripheral Noise

Obviously, you should mute all audio tracks that you don't need before you bounce the tracks that you do need. Less obviously, this also holds true for all of the effects that you don't need. Active Send effects can add background noise even when they aren't receiving input signals.

Backups

When you use track bouncing to combine tracks or lavish on effects, always save the original files first. You'll inevitably come across situations where the composite mix of the tracks isn't satisfactory or the relationship of a dry signal to a wet signal is less than stellar. Backup copies let you reconstruct every arrangement phase in the course of your song and repeat the track bouncing procedure with different settings.

If you avoid these stumbling blocks, you'll be able to use track bouncing to make the most of VST and give yourself a bit more creative leeway for your audio arrangements.

9 Trix for the Mix

To close out the hands-on part of the book, we'll take a look at some of the more common mixdown psychoses, but never fear, therapeutic measures are included free of charge.

Side Effects

A good audio engineer is not inclined to go haywire during mixdown. Maniacal attempts at ›boosting‹ every single sound by EQing it to death, slathering more reverb on each stereo signal to make it even ›roomier,‹ and tormenting each drum sound with a compressor to ›beef it up‹ are in most cases uncool.

Remember, every manipulation that goes above and beyond your primary task just generates undesirable side effects, including additional noise and phase shifting, and will possibly influence transients (impulses).

The Low-Quality VST Filters are a perfect example of what I'm harping on about: These are designed to run on minimum CPU power. The disclaimer ›low-quality‹ should tell you that if you use too many of these during mixdown, you are asking for precisely the kind of side effects mentioned above. the least of your troubles will be a washed-out, thin and limp overall sound.

Try to get the best possible signal in the can during recording. Go easy on EQ bands and effects. During your final mix, if at all possible, restrict yourself to high-quality plug-ins.

Less Is More

Whenever audio engineers and musicians cross swords during mixdown, the word mentioned most often by musicians is ›*More*,‹ usually followed by an unprintable response and then the engineer's resounding ›*No*‹ (unless of course the musician is footing the bill). But seriously, ›Pump it up, give me *more* bass!‹, ›The guitar needs *more* highs!‹, ›The snare needs *more* snap!‹ are routine.

Don't fall into the same trap. During mixdown, newbies are prone to dissect tracks individually and attempt to dial in killer sound for each track rather than look at the big picture. Inevitably, turning up each level as high as it will go and boosting all frequencies achieves this ›killer sound.‹ Every track sounds ›fat,‹ ›warm,‹ ›punchy,‹ but also ›tight‹ and ›bright‹—all at the same time of course. Not, indeed.

You may be skeptical at first, but believe me, if you use this method, you won't come up with the kind of mix that you want! Okay, if you're dealing with ultra-sparse arrangements, you may achieve a tolerable mix, but in all other cases you will end up with mud—indistinct, flabby and totally unappealing.

You don't have an unlimited amount of sonic space in a complex mixdown. If something about the mix irritates you, go for ›less‹ rather than ›more.‹ You'll get to where you want to be much faster.

Frequency Windows

This is another take on the level-boosting mania discussed earlier. You also don't have an unlimited amount of space for frequencies. Think of the frequency spectrum as a line and signals as people standing in it. Everyone needs their bit of breathing room. If you cram too many people too close together, they'll be stepping all over each other:

- You managed to capture a nice fat, low and powerful bass sound in the mix? Congratulations, it's not all that easy! Be happy with what you've got and don't ruin it by boosting the kick drum in the 60 Hz range. You'll be better of if you add some snap at 160 Hz or higher.

- You've ended up with a majestic, wide-body strings sound that covers all angles? Fine, then everyone else can go home. As hard as it may seem, slap the keyboarder's busy left hand away from the keys (in home recording psychology, this is called ›auto-aggressive behavior‹), and while you're at it, lop off some of those highs that are masking the ride cymbal. Now it sounds like you recorded it through a pay phone? Good, we're getting somewhere.

- The guitar player whines on about how his rig sounds so much better in the rehearsal room? Not to worry, it's an occupational hazard, they all do it. If you really want to get nasty, ask him if he also wants the mix to sound like the band in the rehearsal room. This might ring a few bells.

The right settings are always a matter of how complex the mixdown is. There is no such animal as ›the ideal EQ setting for acoustic guitars.‹ It depends entirely on the situation: If you are dealing with a solo performance, plan on adding three more acoustic guitars to the mix or if—fraught with fright—a fearsome foursome is hiding behind the stage curtains. In the latter case (four guitars that is), you will have to filter the individual instruments so they end up higher in the spectrum—they should sound so ›lean‹ that it makes you uncomfortable to listen to them on their own. But you'll get used to it, after all, it's the results that count.

Plotting Sonic Real Estate

Here's another variation on the less-is-more principle: ›Give me *more* space, make it wider!‹

Hold on: The other extreme, that a mix ›isn't spacious enough‹ is universally dreaded. Everybody wants loads of ambient space, depth and 3D feeling. This is why stereo always delivers better results than mono, because ›bigger‹ sounds ›somehow better‹ right?

Nonsense: Think economical when you're positioning signals throughout the stereo soundscape. If you work exclusively with stereo signals, the perspective may be warped. When all of the signals are panned hard left and right, you'll end up with a hole in the center of your mix big enough to drive a truck through. Consider long and hard if a particular signal actually needs all of that much-coveted ›space.‹

There's no law stating that the all stereo signals have to be panned to the outer limits of the stereo image. Even when you're dealing with room reflections simulated by reverb, it's occasionally a good idea to mix them a bit tighter.

For example, if you have recorded several reverb signals—each for a different instrument—via track bouncing, you have discrete access to the panorama settings. Try setting one reverb signal to the ›10 o'clock‹ position (left pan parameter hard right, right pan center) and another to the ›2 o'clock‹ position (left pan parameter center, right hard right). Once the signals are positioned, experiment with different room sizes. In densely layered arrangements with loads of overlapping reflections, this little trick can make the whole thing more transparent.

Finally, a few words of wisdom on the panorama layout. Low frequencies transport a lot of energy, and at the same time, it's hard to put your finger on where they're coming from. Ergo, it doesn't make a bit of sense to pan a low bass sound to a single stereo side. Place low signals such as bass lines or the kick drum dead center, or just slightly off-center if you must. The basic rule of thumb here is: ›The higher a signal is in the frequency spectrum, the more suitable it is for extreme stereo positions.‹

I Am You

And we are altogether. In the realm of home recording, schizophrenia rules. We all wear many different hats—musician, arranger, audio engineer and producer. At the risk of being committed to a closed ward, keep the dialog happening. Talk to each other to come up with the best results.

The point discussed earlier about the frequency windows not only concerns the engineer, but also the arranger. If the arranger complains ›Hey, there's no punch in the bottom end! Crank up the bass!‹, the wily engineer can counter with ›What bass?‹.

As you recall, ›You can't filter something that's not there.‹ First check out your arrangement. Which instrument is the foundation that everything builds on, which instruments are the body, which deliver the shimmering (hopefully) highs? Not until you have an arrangement where each instrument does the job it is supposed to should you start to think about levels and EQing.

10 Faqs

Wizoo Online Support

Updated Book Info

A Web page is dedicated to each book in the Wizoo series. Feel free to check it out for the latest news on the book, new system versions, links to hip Web sites, pages with patches and info.

Punch the following address into your browser:

`http://www.wizoo.com/docs/english/bookservice/vst.htm`

Exploit this information and these resources—you'll save time, meet other like-minded folks and possibly learn a thing or two.

Web Site

If you run into problems that this book can't you help you with, Wizoo offers comprehensive online support on a wide range of topics in the field of electronic sound generation, synthesizers and Midi. When you're in a major hurry to solve a problem, go directly to the ›Wizdom Valley‹ area of our site:

◆ Take a look at our Faqs—here you'll find answers to frequently asked questions on a wide a variety of subjects.

◆ Our link database will help you find other Internet sites that deal with Vst, recording in general and many other topics of interest.

◆ You'll find basic information on and a general introduction to digital audio and related topics in our Newbie Section.

◆ You can also search our Web site for a specific term: Simply click on the ›Search‹ button located on the navigation frame to go to the Search page.

Email

If neither the book nor the Web site can help you find a solution to the problem you're confronted with, feel free to use our free-of-charge trouble-shooting hotline. Email your question to:

Address: mailto:userinput@wizoo.com
Subject: VST <Brief description of the problem>
(e. g. >Your tip doesn't work in my setup<)

Anyone who owns a WIZOO VST guide is welcome to use this service—we do however ask that you do us a favor and stick to these basic prerequisites:

◆ One question per email only.

◆ Keep your email short and to the point.

◆ Please be patient with us, our crew handles up to several hundred questions on peak days.

◆ Bear with us, we're unable to guarantee a comprehensive solution to every problem. With a program as complex as VST, there is always a potential for problems that can't be solved from afar and/or are due to your setup's configuration; in these cases, we'll forward your email to the manufacturer's hotline.

Try to keep these items in mind when you are dropping us a line, and we should be able to help you out.

Maximizing Performance

How can I boost system performance and reliability without spending big bucks on a new computer?
Here are a few tips:

◆ Many older Macintoshes are ready to accept a faster processor as well as other tuning measures. For more info, check the section›Rejuvenating Old Macintoshes‹ on page 48.

- Run a ›lean‹ system: Deactivate all of the peripheral background stuff that you don't need from your Macintosh operating system. Every control panel and system extension forages on performance power and reduces the availability and reliability of your system. Screen savers and any other visual frills are the worst culprits.

- Check out the control panel ›Extensions Manager‹ and set up a bare-bones ›Vsт operating system.‹ See what happens when you restart your Macintosh after you deactivated a control panel or an extension. Apart from the system extension ›Appearance Extension‹ (Mac Os 8.x only) which you should never remove, these experiments under normal circumstances shouldn't cause any serious problems.

In Macintosh magazines, you'll find a detailed list of system components and their function for every Mac Os update. These lists will help you unload excess ›system baggage‹ that can improve performance by up to 20%.

Audio Import and Export

Do I absolutely need a Cᴅ player and audio card with a digital interface to read and import Cᴅ audio data?
No, there is a much easier method. Via special software, Cᴅ audio data can be loaded directly from your computer's Cᴅ-Rᴏм drive and imported to Vsт without signal loss.

Which audio file format is the most universal?
On the Macintosh platform, virtually every audio software can work with Sound Designer II files and many with Aɪꜰꜰ. The latter was the most common format for Macintosh/Pᴄ data exchange for a long time. The Pᴄ standard format Wav is gaining ground, but you still have to use Aɪꜰꜰ files to transport data back and forth between Macintosh and Windows-Pᴄ.

The majority of contemporary audio programs can read and write all essential formats. If you encounter software that doesn't read/write a particular format, utilities are available that convert these special file formats.

How can I swap audio data between Vst and samplers?

You can record the Vst output signal to the sampler and vice versa, preferably via digital interfaces. However, the result is a standard audio recording where editing information is not transported. If your computer and sampler are equipped with Scsi, connect the two via this interface and you will have a versatile, easy-to-handle, all-in-one system.

With the appropriate software, you can send audio files back and forth between Vst and your sampler to your heart's content. Some programs feature this function as a kind of ›encore,‹ e. g. Steinberg ReCycle! or Bias Peak, now a Macintosh standard.

No Audio Output

For some inexplicable reason, the Vst mixer is suddenly silent. What should I do?

Irritatingly, this type of situation can arise even when all of the components are installed properly and everything worked fine just a few minutes ago. Look for the ghost in the machine here:

◆ Make sure that in Vst the item Disable Audio (Options ⇨ Audio Setup) is deactivated. Vst remains in this status until you reset it manually—even if you have quit the program and restarted it.

◆ If you are using a multi I/O card, check if the Vst master signal is routed to the stereo output that you are currently monitoring. Complicated routings, e. g. cascaded Group channels, can cause this type of problem.

◆ If you are using a half-duplex card, you have to deactivate the audio inputs to enable audio output.

- In some situations, for instance if the system has to deal with way too much data (Cpu overload due to an excess of effects or automation data), the Vst audio system gets a case of the ›hiccups‹ and obstinately refuses to cooperate. Try the command Reset Devices in the Options menu.

- If none of these measures work, quit the program and restart it.

Audio Crackless or Program Crashes

Vst generates unusually conspicuous crackles, hissing or other undesirable noise during audio recording or playback. What should I do?

In this case, you should first take a gander at Vst's performance display (Panels ⇨ Audio Performance) and ensure it is in the green zone. If your system isn't pushing the performance limits and was working fine just a little while ago, you may have encountered a system ›hiccup‹ discussed in the previous paragraph. Try the suggested trouble-shooting measures.

There are two primary error sources when cracking noises or crashes become routine occurrences:

Conflicts with Graphics Cards Drivers

If you are using a third-party vendor's graphics card, its driver can be culprit behind audio problems and system crashes. Look here first:

- Check if the problems occur more often when you change numerous elements on your screen. If this is indeed the case, the problem is definitely connected to your graphics card driver.

- Obtain the latest driver for your graphics card, via Internet is the fastest way.

♦ Check if the hardware acceleration function is activated in the graphics card driver. If so, reset this parameter to zero and see what happens.

♦ Insert the graphics card and audio card (provided you have one) in Pci slots that are as far apart as possible.

Scsi Stress

Please read through the section ›Scsi System‹ on page 38. The Scsi bus can cause unique problems:

♦ Ultra Wide and other high-end Scsi controllers can obstruct the Pci bus and thus—in combination with Pci audio cards such as the Korg 1212-I/O or Event Gina/Darla—cause cracking noises. In this case, reduce Pci data throughput to 10 Mb/s via the Scsi controller's configuration software.

Pci slots are usually managed on the mainboard in groups of three (segments). Two powerful Pci cards (graphics and sound) in a threesome often causes ego problems. In mainboards equipped with six and more Pci slots, you can generally counteract the problem by installing the two Pci cards in separate groups, in other words, as far apart as they will go. For this reason, you should only install a high-speed Scsi controller along with a Pci audio card if you own one of the relatively uncommon Macintoshes equipped with more than three Pci slots.

After I start Vst, it issues strange error messages or won't start at all although it worked just fine the last time I worked with it. What gives?

Macintosh software tends to sulk when Vst or another program crashed and punishes you by refusing to cooperate the next time you want to work with it. All kinds of settings go up in virtual smoke when this happens—but with the right overtures, it will eventually forgive and forget:

- **Preferences:** Open the Cubase Preferences folder (under System Folder ⇨ Preferences) and drag the its entire content to another position where you can be sure of finding it later. At the next program start, VST generates all preset files anew, which will often take care of the problem.

  Keep in mind however that this measure wipes out internal program presets. You'll have to reset these manually or try to copy—one at a time—the files back that you moved earlier.

- **Sound Manager:** If you are using VST with the Macintosh audio hardware and suddenly the sound of silence is all that the audio will give you (or all kinds of initialization complaints come your way at program start-up), you can usually blame the Sound Manager. Open the appropriate control panels, e. g. Monitors and Sound and try changing some of these parameters. If this won't work, try deleting the corresponding Preferences files (Sound Preferences and Monitors and Sound Preferences ⇨ SoundInPrefs and SoundOutPrefs).

- **PRAM:** The so-called parameter RAM is a computer component that saves certain Mac OS presets. If this is faulty, crashes will occur regularly. To delete this memory and re-initialize it, you have to press and hold the key combination ⌘⌥PR until the system start signal sounds a second time.

- The so-called ›**Desktop file**,‹ in which the Macintosh saves links between files and symbols, should be deleted every couple of weeks—your Macintosh will feel all the better for it. The computer doesn't do this automatically and the data heap grows and grows, which of course doesn't do much for the speed and operating reliability of your box.

  To regenerate the Desktop file, press and hold the key combination ⌘⌥ when you start the computer and answer the queries that pop up.

Appendix

Cᴅ-Rᴏᴍ Table of Contents

Data Section

Folder	Contents
Tutorial	Example songs 02 through 40 in Vsᴛ format, Wizoo Windows Sets folder (preprogrammed window configurations for the Vsᴛ example songs)
VST Demo	Steinberg Cubase Vsᴛ 4.0 Macintosh demo, other folders with ›accessories‹ (e. g. Vsᴛ instructions in Pᴅꜰ format, Mixer Maps, Templates etc.)
sonicWORX Artist Basic PPC	Prosoniq sonicWorx Artist Basic Pᴘᴄ (fully functional newbie version of the Audio Editor series)
ProTools 3.4	Digidesign ProTools 3.4 (fully functional version of the Audio Editor/ Multitrack Recording Software; runs up to sixteen tracks with Macintosh audio hardware)
Acrobat Reader 3.01	Adobe Acrobat Reader (for opening, viewing and printing Pᴅꜰ files, e. g. the Vsᴛ instructions)
Browser	The current versions of the Internet browsers Netscape Communicator 4.05 and Microsoft Internet Explorer 4.01
OMS 2.3.4	Opcode Oᴍs (current version of the standard Mɪᴅɪ management system for Macintosh)
Sound App 2.5	Standard audio freeware for Macintosh (Audio converter supporting many formats)

Folder	Contents
Snd Sampler 3.5.2	Standard audio shareware for Macintosh (audio recorder/player with many edit functions)
Free plug-ins	Shareware and freeware plug-ins for VST Macintosh by Dave Brown, Stefan Sprenger and Vellocet
Wizoo	WIZOO Catalog and VST Internet links (HTML files; you need an Internet browser to open these)

Audio Tracks

Track	Description	Comments	Page
01	Data track! Do not play this track on an audio CD player!	Some CD players do not indicate this track on the display. In this case, successive track numbers are offset by one.	—
02	A major chord consisting of 4 sine tones: A = 220 Hz, C# = 293 Hz, E = 348 Hz, A = 440 Hz	Sine tones are critical test material and thus may sound exceptionally noisy via low-cost audio cards.	89
03	Chord from 02 with emphasis on each sine tone via EQ gain	See Track 2	89
04	Original mixdown	*	91
05	Example 04 with different EQ settings: ♦ EQ_1: +Gain 8, Freq. 73 Hz, Q 0.55 ♦ EQ_2: Gain +12.9, Freq. 13450 Hz, Q 0.54 ♦ EQ_3: Gain −12, Freq. 805 Hz, Q 0.66 ♦ EQ_4: Gain +12.2, Freq. 2008 Hz, Q 0.55 ♦ EQ_5: Gain +15.1, Freq. 3350 Hz, Q 0.7		91
06	Original hihat		92
07	Example 06 EQ bands activated successively at octave intervals		92
08	Original drum loop	Excerpt from WIZOO CD-ROM ›Hamburg Loopz‹**	92
09	Example 08 Kick drum with EQ gain faded out	see 08	92

Track	Description	Comments	Page
10	Original drum loop	Excerpt from Wɪᴢᴏᴏ Cᴅ-Rᴏᴍ ›Hamburg Loopz‹**	92
11	Example 10 Eǫ Separation and effects	Left (kick drum) Grungelizer, right (hihat) stereo echo	92
12	Mono strings	Jᴅ-800	93
13	Example 12 Pseudo stereo via Eǫ processing	Listen to 12 and 13 alternately via headphones!	93
14	Original e-piano	Roland Jᴅ-800	104
15	Example 14 with serial effects	Chorus + Grungelizer	104
16	Original synth arpeggio	Access Virus	105
17	Example 16 with parallel effects	2 × Delay + Auto Panner	105
18	Left/right test file	Check it the image is correct on both sides.	116
19	Example 18 with stereo in/out plug-in (Grungelizer)	Effect signal on both sides	117
20	Example 18 with mono in/stereo out plug-in (Espacial)	The ›binaural impression‹ of the effects signal is heard best via headphones.	117
21	Example 18 with mono in/out plug-in (FuzzBox)	The ›monaural impression‹ of the effects signal is heard best via headphones.	118
22	Original electric guitar	Roland Vɢ-8	124
23	Example 22 with tremolo effect and reverb	Auto Pan insert and WunderVerb 3 send	124
24	Original voice		125
25	Example 24 with self-resonance via chorus a) high Time value + low Lғᴏ frequency b) medium Time value + low Lғᴏ frequency c) medium Time value + high Lғᴏ frequency	Choirus insert	125
26	Original synth line	Clavia Nord Lead	127
27	Example 26 with slight FuzzBox distortion	The effect is deliberately subtle. Listen to and compare Examples 26 and 27.	127

Track	Description	Comments	Page
28	Original percussion		128
29	Example 29 with short delay/feedback (approx. 10 and 20 ms)	Stereo delay as send	128
30	Original vocals		136
31	Example 31 with compression simulated via dynamic volume events		136
32	Original synth staccato	Access Virus	137
33	Example 32 with panning effect via dynamic panorama events		138
34	Original drum loop	Excerpt from WIZOO CD-ROM ›Lofi Junkiez‹**	140
35	Example 35 with dynamic effects and EQ automation		140
36	Original snare		150
37	Example 37 with gated reverb	Reverb imported via track bouncing	150
38	Example 37 with reverse reverb	Reverb imported via track bouncing	151
39	Original vocals + chords		151
40	Example 39 with reverb + serial delay reverb on vocals	Delay imported via track bouncing	151

* Excerpts from my songs—commercial duplication and distribution prohibited.

** The WIZOO CD-ROMs ›Hamburg Loopz‹ and ›Lofi Junkiez‹ are available as special Macintosh/Windows CD-ROMs for direct VST audio import.

Cubase VST Internet Links

Check out the Book Support page at the WIZOO Web site for a regularly updated list of VST links.

We've compiled a bunch of links to Web sites that provide information, updates, contacts and FAQs on Cubase VST and related topics. We've commented on the majority of sites to give you a rough idea of what to expect.

The fastest way to go to these sites is to simply open the file vstlinks.htm on the Cd-Rom via your browser and click directly on the links listed there.

Steinberg Internet Sites

Steinberg Worldwide: http://www.steinberg-us.com/

Steinberg North America: http://www.us-steinberg.net/

Steinberg Germany: http://www.steinberg.de/
German Web site of the Hamburg-based software maker featuring news and information on as well as support and service for Cubase. The company maintains its own Ftp server for fast downloading. First place to go to for users in Germany.

Steinberg Francais: http://www.steinberg.fr/index.html

Steinberg Italia: http://www.midiware.com/steinberg/index.html

Steinberg Knowledge Base:
http://service.steinberg.de/sc/knowledge.nsf
Steinberg's own informative and indispensable pages featuring Faqs. Many, many Q & A's on Cubase Vst. Quick help for the most common problems—and here's the good thing—at any time day or night.

Create Synced Midimixer Maps: http://www.steinberg-us.com/support/user/creasym2/ecreate.htm
Lots of scoop on Steinberg's Cubase and mixer maps. A good place to go for newbies!

Info

Cubase for Windows Users:
http://www.instanet.com/~thedusk/

Here you'll find a load of tricks and tips even for Macintosh users and lots of info on plug-ins, the Cubase Clubs—coveted mixer maps are also available here.

Cubase Club: http://www.instanet.com/~thedusk/club_cubase/club_cubase.html

Cubase Mailing List:
http://www.instanet.com/~thedusk/subscribe.html

Here you can subscribe to the Cubase mailing list and talk to like-minded folks every day for the rest of your natural-born life.

The Cubase Archive: ftp://ftp.mcc.ac.uk/pub/music/cubase/

Not exactly up to the minute, but still worth a look for Cubase devotees. Served up luke-warm: FAQs, mixer maps, drum maps and historic demo versions.

VST 3.5 Pc Performance Survey:
http://www.padworld.demon.co.uk/vst.html

Macintosh Hard- and Software

Apple Technical Information Library:
http://www.til.info.apple.com/

Comprehensive technical information on Apple hardware and software. A good tip when you come across puzzling computer and operating system problems.

Apple Mac Os: http://www.apple.com/macos/

Updates and trouble-shooting for Mac Os.

Every Mac: http://www.everymac.com/bymanufacturer.html

Catalog of all Apple Macintosh's and Macintosh-compatible clones.

MacintoshOs:
http://www.MacintoshOS.com/macintosh.museum/index.shtml
A list of all Macintoshes and clones.

MacShare: http://www.macshare.com/
Nice grab-bag of Macintosh shareware.

Steinberg: http://metalguru.steinberg.de/sc/knowledge.nsf/
RefIK/compatibility_chart1
Steinberg's current list of Vst-tested and approved computer models.

Audio Hardware

The following is a list of Web sites where you can get in-depth information on the audio systems discussed in this book:

Creamware: http://www.creamware.com/
Tdat 8, Tdat 16

Digidesign: http://www.digidesign.com/prod/
Audiomedia 3, ProTools III/24

Event Electronics: http://www.event1.com/
Darla, Gina, Layla

Korg: http://www.korg.com/sndlnk1.htm
1212 I/O

Lexicon: http://www.lexicon.com/Studio/homeframe.htm
Lexicon Studio System

Lucid: http://www.lucidtechnology.com/
Pci24, Nb24 and Ada converters

Marc of the Unicorn: http://www.motu.com/
Motu 2408

Sonorus: http://www.sonorus.com/
StudI/O

Yamaha: http://www.yamaha.co.jp/product/proaudio/
homeenglish/dsfact/ds2416/index.htm
DSP Factory

Other Audio Software

VST Macintosh can do a lot, but not everything. Here's a brief run-down of Macintosh audio software that is especially well-suited for use with VST:

Bias: http://www.bias-inc.com/
Peak, Peak Le

Digidesign: http://www.digidesign.com/prod/ptpm/
ProTools software (Power Mix version)

Propellerheads: http://www.propellerheads.se/
ReCycle 1.6 (Drumloop Editor with special VST export format) and Rebirth 2.0 (the ultimate virtual drum machine for VST).

Prosoniq: http://www.prosoniq.com/
sonicWorx Artist, sonicWorx Studio, sonicWorx Power Bundle (audio editors with innovative editing options)

Steinberg: http://www.steinberg.net/products/index.html
Reseller for ReCycle and Rebirth (see above: Propellerheads)

VST Plug-ins

To add to the plug-ins on the CD-ROM, you can stock up your supply of Cubase plug-ins at the following sites. Some are free and others commercial (= pay before you plug-n-play), but if you want to be sure that you invest in the right plug-ins, we recommend that you check out our ›Wizoo Guide Cubase Vst Plug-ins‹ (catalog and order form are located at the end this book).

Antares: http://www.antares-systems.com/
   Auto-Tune Vst

Arboretum: http://www.arboretum.com/
   Hyperprism, Vst/Hyperprism Dx

Dave Brown: http://www.dbrown.force9.co.uk/
   Sweep Delay, Tempo Delay, Tremolo, ProDelay

Duy: http://www.duy.es/
   Duy Shape, Max Duy, Duy Wide, DaD Valve

Neurosoniq: http://www.trust-group.com/neuro.home.e.htm
   Groove Delay

Object Productions: http://gate.cruzio.com/~object/
   Vintage Power Pak Vol 1, Power Insert Pack

Opcode: http://www.opcode.com/
   Vocoder, Vinyl (Vst Macintosh version in the works)

Prosoniq: http://www.prosoniq.com/
   Voxciter, Roomulator, Ambisone, Dynasone

Spectral Design: http://www.spectral-design.com/
   DeClicker, DeNoiser, Loudness Maximizer, Magneto, Red Valve-It, Free-D, Free Filter, Q-Metric

Spl: http://www.spl-electronics.com/
   De-Esser

Stefan Sprenger: http://www.prosoniq.com/sms/sprenger.html
   North Pole

Steinberg: http://www.steinberg-us.com/
   Loudness Maximizer, Magneto, Spectralizer, DeClicker, DeNoiser

Tc works: http://www.tcworks.de/
   Tc Native Reverb

Vellocet: http://www.cs.uwa.edu.au/~skot/vellocet/
software.html
   VPingPong, VFlanger, VNoPhones

Waldorf: http://www.waldorf-gmbh.de/waldorf/index.html
   D-Pole

Waves: http://www.waves.com/
   Native Power Pack with True Verb, C1 Compressor/Gate,
   Q10 ParaGraphic Eq, L1 Ultra Maximizer, S1 Stereo Imager.
   Furthermore: AudioTrack VST, Maxx Bass, DeEsser, Paz,
   Renaissance Compressor.

Glossary

This glossary deals primarily with terms, abbreviations and
acronyms mentioned in passing in the book, but due to space
constraints, weren't explained in detail. There are also a
number of terms that you will come across when you are
configuring and working with VST. If you can't find a term
you're looking for here, check the index.

AD converters—Short for ›analog/digital;‹ a device that con-
verts an analog signal to a digital signal that represents
equivalent information via sampling.

   Adat—Digital 8-track audio recorder based on video tape
by Alesis; the standard device in its class; diverse generations and models are available.

   Adat Optical—Optical interface for parallel transmission of
eight audio channels via fiber-optic cable. Now the established standard for digital multi-channel interfaces.

   AES/EBU—Short for ›Audio Engineering Society/European
Broadcast Union;‹ this is the association's standard trans-
mission format for professional stereo digital audio signals
The format is similar to ⇨S/P-DIF, but uses balanced line

drivers at a higher voltage. Depending on the type of devices involved, AES/EBU and S/P-DIF coax interfaces can communicate directly.

Amplitude—Amplitude is a term used to describe the amount of a signal. It can relate to volume in an audio signal or the amount of voltage in an electrical signal. In the audio sector, the term is often equated with ›level‹ and ›volume.‹

ASIO—Short for ›Audio Stream Input Output,‹ VST's own software interface to a variety of audio cards.

Audio file—A file that actually contains digital audio data, as opposed to ⇨audio regions or audio segments.

Audio region—This simulated audio file holds the place for an actual ⇨audio file or portions thereof; it doesn't contain audio data, only peripheral information such as the start and end point.

Aux—Short for auxiliary; in mixers, these circuits are usually identical to effects sends.

Bus—In computer jargon, this general term refers to data, address and control circuits. The term describes the circuits via which the ⇨CPU communicates with peripheral devices and expansion cards (⇨PCI, ⇨Nubus).

Bus width—Refers to the maximum number of bits that can be transported via the ⇨bus simultaneously, i. e. the de facto number of parallel circuits.

CD audio—Short for ›Compact Disc—Audio;‹ current standard for stereo music CDs: 44.1 kHz ⇨sampling rate and 16-bit word width.

CD-R—Short for ›CD-Recordable;‹ The term describes a blank CD. It is placed in a ⇨CD-R recorder to burn digital data onto the CD (cannot be deleted/overwritten).

CD-R recorder—Also called ›CD burner‹ or ›toaster;‹ device used to burn data onto CD-Rs, can also usually be used as a CD-ROM drive.

CD-RW—Short for ›CD-ReWritable;‹ Similar to ⇨CD-R, although here data can be deleted and overwritten. CD-RW recorders and discs are still relatively expensive.

Clock—Frequency specification (usually in MHz) that describes how fast the computer can execute certain operations. The specification for processors is the most widely-known clock type; it pertains to the computing cycle of the ⇨Cpu. ⇨Bus clock is also crucial to ⇨performance; it describes at which rate the Cpu can communicate with other computer components via the busses.

Color depth—Determines how many different colors a computer's graphical system can (and should) display simultaneously. Standard values are 8 bits (256 colors/Low Color), 16 bits (thousands of colors/High Color) and 32 bits (millions colors/True Color). High values give good visuals, but require a great deal of computing performance.

Comb filter—Filter curve with steep notches, which in a graphical representation, resemble the teeth of a comb. Changes the timbre of a sound drastically and is usually considered an undesirable side effect caused by ⇨phase shifting, among others.

Cpu—Short for ›Central Processing Unit;‹ the main processor that is primarily responsible for the overall performance of the computer.

Da converter—Short for ›digital/analog converter;‹ a device that changes an analog signal into a digital signal that represents equivalent information via ⇨sampling.

dB—Short for ›decibel;‹ a numerical expression for the relative (a logarithmic value) loudness of a sound. Different measures of dB such as dB u or dB V are used depending on the application and nominal value.

Destructive—›Destructive audio processing‹ means that the actual audio data in an ⇨audio file are changed as opposed to just editing peripheral or playback parameters.

Dimm—Short for ›Dual In-line Memory Module;‹ board equipped with ⇨Ram memory components; it is plugged into appropriate ⇨slots on the mainboard.

Disk At Once—⇨Cd-R recorder mode: All tracks are written to the ⇨Cd-R without interruption. This mode is generally required to write on Cds in ⇨Cd audio format. Not all Cd-R recorders can operate in this mode (⇨Track At Once).

Dma—Short for ›Direct Memory Access;‹ here data transport operations between system components are executed without the help of the Cpu (⇨Busmaster cards).

Dsp—Short for ›Digital Signal Processor,‹ a computer chip designed specifically for computing audio data. This type of chip is installed in some audio cards for computing effects and related data without the help of the Cpu.

Duplex—This term goes way back to the days of the telegraph. Today in the context of audio cards, duplex mode refers to parallel operation of audio inputs and outputs. Half-duplex means that an audio card does not support simultaneous recording and playback operation. Full-duplex means that you can use inputs and outputs simultaneously.

Dvd—Short for ›Digital Versatile Disk,‹ a format that is the designated successor to contemporary Cds (⇨Cd audio). These disks hold video and audio data. With massive storage capacity of seventeen gigabyte (equivalent to 25 conventional Cds); the format for audio Dvd is 24 bits/96 kHz.

E-Ide—Short for ›Enhanced ⇨Ide;‹ which is exactly what it actually is.

Fpu—Short for ›Floating Point Unit;‹ a computer component, subroutine or algorithm that executes floating point calculations. These operations are crucial in real-time audio computing.

Full-duplex—⇨Duplex.

Gain—In audio jargon, this term is equivalent to level. For filters, it describes the degree of boost/cut in ⇨dB.

Half-duplex—⇨Duplex.

Hfs—›Hierarchical File System;‹ the standard file system of Mac Os.

Hfs+—Upgrade of Hfs introduced with Mac Os 8.1. Most important improvement: Hfs+ ensures that small files take up less space on a storage medium. Hfs+ is not recommended for audio hard disk. Rather than bringing benefits, it usually causes problems. Current Mac Os versions support Hʀs and Hʀs+ formatted media; you can even run them on the same system.

IDE—Short for ›Integrated Device Electronics,‹ a ⇨bus used to connect Iᴅᴇ-compatible devices such as or Cᴅ-Rᴏᴍ drives. The newer standards are Fast Aᴛᴀ 2, Aᴛᴀᴘɪ and ⇨E-Iᴅᴇ.

I/O—Short for ›Input/Output.‹

Latency—Delay between audio and Mɪᴅɪ in the Vsᴛ audio system; highest latency in Mᴍᴇ operation, lowest with an Asɪᴏ direct interface.

LTC—Short for ›Longitudinal Time Code‹—Synchronization signal for video links that is recorded to a video tape along with images (⇨Vɪᴛᴄ).

Mac Os—Short ›Macintosh Operating System.‹

Non-destructive — ›Non-destructive audio processing‹ means that the actual audio data in an ⇨audio file are not edited, only peripheral or playback parameters such as ⇨regions and segments.

Nubus—Outdated bus format for expansion slots in Macintosh computers. Older models have up to six Nubus slots. The current standard bus format is ⇨Pᴄɪ.

PCI—Short for ›Peripheral Component Interface;‹ Intel ⇨bus standard.

PCI bridge—Controller chip via which the Pᴄɪ bus communicates with the Cᴘᴜ. In Macintosh-compatible computers with more than three slots, used as a link to the diverse Pᴄɪ trios.

PDS—Short for ›Processor Direct Slot,‹ a slot in many older Macintosh models that is connected directly to the Cᴘᴜ. It can often be used for a processor upgrade in these models.

Performance—Overall computing power determined by the ⇨Cᴘᴜ, ⇨clock, ⇨Rᴀᴍ and ⇨bus, among other factors.

Phase—Also called ›phase position‹ or ›phase angle;‹ specified in 0 to 360..It describes an attribute of an oscillation that is especially significant when signals overlap.

Plug-in—Modular expansion software that enhance the capabilities of another program. The internal effects in Vsт Macintosh can be upgraded with plug-ins in the requisite format.

Power Macintosh—General term for Apple Macintosh computers equipped with a Ppc Processor.

PPQ—Short for ›Pulses Per Quarter;‹ determines how many increments a quarter note is divided into; essential for sequencer timing, among others.

RAM—Short for ›Random Access Memory.‹ This is the memory that handles your working data; its capacity is expressed in Mʙ (megabyte). Normally this memory is ›volatile,‹ which means that the contents are only saved for as long as the device is powered up.

Routing—Generally refers to how a signal is sent through signal circuits; is often used to describe specific input and output ›assignments.‹

Run-time discrepancy—Minimal delay of audio signals, usually in the millisecond range. Generally not a huge problem expect for in signals that are linked directly (e. g. the two channels in a stereo recording). In this case, these differences generate ⇨phase shifting and ⇨comb filter effects.

Sample rate—Also called sampling frequency. The term describes the frequency at which analog audio material is sampled.

Sample rate converter—Device or algorithm that translates one ⇨sample rate into another; this conversion always leads to some type timing problem—the quantizing goes out of whack, which degrades the audio quality.

SDRAM—›Synchronous Dynamic Random Access Memory;‹ a special type of D⇨RAM. In addition to conventional control signals, it works with a clock signal for faster access. SDRAM is used in Apple's current G3 computers.

SIMM—Short for ›Single In-line Memory Module;‹ board with ⇨RAM modules that is plugged into the corresponding ⇨slots on the computer's mainboard.

Slot—General term for expansion ports on the computer's mainboard.

S/P-DIF—Short for ›Sony/Philips Digital InterFace;‹ standard format for transporting digital audio data. Either an optical or a coaxial interface, depending on the type of device. The format is similar to ⇨AES/EBU, although it features unbalanced circuits and lower voltages. Nevertheless, AES/EBU and S/P-DIF coax interface can often communicate directly (depending on the type of devices involved).

TDIF—Short for ›Tascam Digital Interface Format;‹ a digital 8-channel interface that is primarily used for connecting digital multi-track recorder (DTR) by Tascam.

Terminator—In an ⇨SCSI bus, the first and last device in the chain have to be equipped with an activated terminating resistor, the circumspectly-named ›terminator.‹ Available either as a software switch or external plug that fits the SCSI port.

Track At Once—⇨CD-R recorder mode: Each track is written individually to the ⇨CD-R. The laser that is doing the writing is switched off at the end of a track and switched on again at the start of the next track (⇨Disk At Once).

Transients—extremely brief signal peaks, for instance a kick drum impulse with a great deal of ›click.‹

USB—›Universal Serial Bus;‹ Intel-sponsored standard for communication between computers and peripherals. The serial circuit between devices via a single, low-cost cable slows data transport down, so it is unsuitable for audio hard disks. First integrated in an Apple computer with the release of iMac.

VRAM—Short for ›Video Random Access Memory;‹ fast memory on graphics cards for buffering screen contents.

Wordclock—Clock signal required by digital audio interfaces to ensure the ⇨sampling rates of the connected devices run in absolute sync.

And This Year's Wizoo Winners Are ...

...Tom Wendt, Manfred Rürup, Charlie Steinberg, Stefan Scheffler as well as the entire Steinberg crew for innovation, gracious support and unveiling what's behind the curtain,

Gisela Derichs for tutorial vocals and friendly support of the author in times of authorial travail,

René Algesheimer for Wizoo shareware tips and links,

Peter Gorges as ›The Big Wizoo‹ for suggesting this book and—on the lighter side of life—providing hilarious email correspondence.

Appendix

Index

Index

Other Wizoo Guides and CD-Roms

On the following pages, you'll find an excerpt from our growing book and CD-Rom Catalog.

Be sure to check out the latest updates to the book and CD-Rom program at our Web site at http://www.wizoo.com/.

Feel free to order any of the wonderful Wizoo products via the coupon at the end of the book by credit card.

All Wizoo Guides are available in English and German versions.

Wizoo Guides

Ralf Kleinermanns: Wizoo Guide Vst Plug-Ins

► Reviews, Ratings, Tips and Tricks.

This book will help you find the right plug-ins for your purposes. Reviews, ratings and tips on all commercial and freeware plug-ins for Windows and Macintosh users.

► Including CD-Rom Win/Mac featuring demos of all plug-ins

Order no.	Price	Isbn
WizLH00007E	27.90 Us $	3-927954-33-0

Available in autumn of 1998 the know-how upgrade for the Wizoo Guide Cubase

Dave Bellingham/Peter Gorges: **Wizoo Guide Kawai K5000**

▶ Introduction to Add Synthesis, Sound Design, Tips and Tricks

The programmers handbook for all K5000 users featuring insider know-how, tips, tricks and many examples of advanced additive synthesis.

▶ Including disk with patch examples and samples for SoundDiver

Order no.	Price	Isbn
Wizlh00001E	27.90 Us $	3-927954-21-7

Peter Gorges: **Wizoo Guide Nord Modular**

▶ Introduction, Modular Sound Synthesis, Virtual Assembly Instructions

The manual for everyone who owns a Modular or is interested in it—how to assemble a virtual synthesizer and make the most of it and its modules, audio-in and sequencers.

▶ Including Cd-Rom (Audio/Win) with audio clips and patch examples

Order no.	Price	Isbn
Wizlh00002E	27.90 Us $	3-927954-23-3

Udo Weyers: **Wizoo Guide Roland Jv/Xp**

▶ Sounds and Sequencing, Tips and Tricks, Buyers Guide for Synths and Expansions.

The book for all Jv/Xp users who want to find out how to make the most of this synthesizer. Including buyer's guide and an overview of models. For Jv-80/880/90/1000/1080/2080 and Xp-50/60/80.

▶ Including Cd-Rom with audio demos and shareware

Order no.	Price	Isbn
Wizlh00003E	27.90 Us $	3-927954-25-X

René Algesheimer: **Top 30 Music Shareware**

▶ The Best ›Soft‹ synths, Audio Editors, Sequencers, Utilities

In this book, we'll introduce you to the 30 best music shareware programs—all of which are every bit as good as their costly commercial counterparts. If you're musically ambitious or just want to ›check stuff out,‹ this book is a great place to start and whichever way you approach it, we're sure you'll have big time fun while you're at it.

▶ Including Cd-Rom with all shareware titles covered

Order no.	Price	Isbn
Wizlh00005E	27.90 Us $	3-927954-29-2

Thomas Adam/Peter Gorges: **Wizoo Guide Fx**

▶ The Best Effects Settings for Sound Design and Mixing

We'll show you how to make the most of your effects and put some sparkle into your sounds. Hundreds of presets for all effects types. Copy and edit at will!

▶ Including Cd Win/Mac/Audio with demos of all effects

Order no.	Price	Isbn
Wizlh00006E	27.90 Us $	3-927954-31-4

Ralf Kleinermanns: **Wizoo Guide Vst Windows**

Find out all about the best hardware for the job, how to boost the program's performance and make the most of plug-ins, Eqs and mixer automation; plus a mother-lode of professional mixing, mastering and routing tips.

▶ Including Cd-Rom Win/Audio with examples, shareware- und freeware plug-ins

Order no.	Price	Isbn
Wizlh00004E	27.90 Us $	3-927954-27-6

Cd-Roms

Claudius Brüse & Peter Gorges:
T-Rex primeval electronic power

T-Rex features a Jurassic zoo of electronic and techno patches originally created on dinosaur synths. Add some primeval power to your library and feel the earth move after you load these sounds to your sampler.

Format	Order no.	Price
Akai S1000 and compatible	Wizsc00001C	49.90 Us $
Wav, Aiff, SoundFont	Wizsc00001P	44.90 Us $

Michael Mühlhaus & Bernhard Reiss: **Hamburg Loopz**

► sophisticated german loops & samples

›Hamburg Loopz‹ is not just another generic loop Cd, it is a musical soup du jour of the finest electronic loops and drum sets that ever graced your table. With a menu chock full of slamming grooves for your editing pleasure. 84 to 194 bpm.

Format	Order no.	Price
Akai S1000 and compatible	Wizsc00002C	49.90 Us $
Wav, Aiff	Wizsc00002P	27.90 Us $

Frank Heiss/Dr. Walker: **lofi junkies volume one**

► phucked up trashcanfunk

Totally phucked up but phunk.eee Triphop-, Hip-Hop-, Big-Beat- & Breakbeat Drumloops from the cologne underground for the global underground.

Format	Order no.	Price
Akai S1000 and compatible	Wizsc00003C	49.90 Us $
Wav, Aiff	Wizsc00003P	27.90 Us $

Johannes Waehneldt: **Magnetica**

► ... only the best survived.

The legendary electromagnetic keyboards in size Xxxl on a single Cd-Rom: Rhodes Mk II, Suitcase Rhodes, Wurlitzer Piano, Hohner Clavinet, Hammond B3 Organ.

Format	Order no.	Price
Akai S3000/5000/6000	Wizsc00004C	49.90 Us $

Peter Gorges: **Wizoo powered Wave**

► ... Pure plugged power...

Peter Gorges manhandled the Waldorf Wave and made it do things even the designer hadn't thought possible. Up to sixteen oscillators worked overtime to pump out each note! The outcome: fatter-than-George Foreman, heavier-than-plutonium, tighter-than-Spandex.

Format	Order no.	Price
Akai S3000/5000/6000	Wizsc00005C	49.90 Us $

Peter Gorges: **Wizoo powered Nord**

► ... small, hot, & red: The real chili pepper!

This hot tamale makes other digital takes on analog sounds look like refried beans. Complete synthesizer modules with 128 analog sounds for samplers and soundcards.

Format	Order no.	Price
Akai S3000/5000/6000	Wizsc00006C	49.90 Us $

Peter Gorges: **Wizoo powered Dx**

► ... sines of the time

The best Fm sounds by the best Fm synth. If you always wanted to own a Dx or just want to find out what it is capable of, this is the Cd-Rom for you.

Format	Order no.	Price
Akai S3000/5000/6000	Wizsc00007C	49.90 Us $

Other Wizoo Guides and CD-Roms

This is how you order:

Online
Visit our Web site
http://www.wizoo.com/
At WIZOO, you can fill up your online shopping cart with goodies such as books and CD-ROMS and order them via credit card, fax or email.

Telephone
Call our MM shop at
+49 2236 96217-25.

Fax
Fax the coupon to us at +49 2236 96217-5.

Mail
Mail the coupon to us at:
WIZOO
An der Wachsfabrik 8
D 50996 Cologne
Germany

Email
Send an email with your order to us at:
shoporder@wizoo.com

(: wizoo :)

Item No.	Item	Quantity	Price	
(:	:) (:	:) (:	:) (:	:)
(:	:) (:	:) (:	:) (:	:)
(:	:) (:	:) (:	:) (:	:)
(:	:) (:	:) (:	:) (:	:)
(:	:) (:	:) (:	:) (:	:)
		Shipping	(:	:)
		SUM	(:	:)

Creditcard VISA ( ) American Express ( ) Eurocard ( )
valid thru (:   :) Cardholder (:   :)
Card Number (:   :)

Shipping and Handling
European Countries: Add 4.00 DM (2.50 US $) for each item, orders over 100.00 DM (60.00 US $) are shipped free of charge.
Other Countries: Add 8.00 DM (5.00 US $) for each item, orders over 200.00 DM (120.00 US $) are shipped free of charge.

Last Name/Name

Street No./Street Name

Suburb/Town & ZIP

State/Region & Country

Telephone

Date/Signature

Other WIZOO Guides and CD-ROMS

Wizoo Guide

Cubase Vst Macintosh